W9-DGT-086

The Essential TV Director's Handbook

WITHDRAWN

WITHDRAWN

The Essential TV Director's Handbook

Peter Jarvis

 focal press

Focal Press
An imprint of Butterworth-Heinemann
Linacre House, Jordan Hill, Oxford OX2 8DP
225 Wildwood Avenue, Woburn, MA 01801-2041
A division of Reed Educational and Professional Publishing Ltd

℞ A member of the Reed Elsevier plc group

OXFORD   BOSTON   JOHANNESBURG
MELBOURNE   NEW DELHI   SINGAPORE

First published 1998

© Peter Jarvis 1998

All rights reserved. No part of this publication may be reproduced in
any material form (including photocopying or storing in any medium by
electronic means and whether or not transiently or incidentally to some
other use of this publication) without the written permission of the
copyright holder except in accordance with the provisions of the Copyright,
Designs and Patents Act 1988 or under the terms of a licence issued by the
Copyright Licensing Agency Ltd, 90 Tottenham Court Road, London,
England W1P 9HE. Applications for the copyright holder's written
permission to reproduce any part of this publication should be addressed
to the publishers

British Library Cataloguing in Publication Data
A catalogue record for this book is available from the British Library

Library of Congress Cataloguing in Publication Data
A catalogue record for this book is available from the Library of Congress

ISBN 0 2405 1503 X

Printed and bound in Great Britain by
Biddles Limited, Guildford and King's Lynn

Contents

Introduction

I remember one wet evening in an Amsterdam hotel room enjoying a drink or two with a television crew. It was the end of a hard day. One of us was idly switching between the dozen or so TV channels on offer. Suddenly the screen was filled with writhing limbs and gynaecological detail. Orgasmic moans filled the room. We had hit upon a porno channel at a time, not very long ago, when nothing like it would be seen on British screens, even in a hotel.

There were a range of possible reactions available to us, boggle-eyed astonishment, wet lipped fascination, contempt and derision, embarrassment, or moral outrage. What combination of these feelings were felt by my colleagues for the first couple of dumbstruck minutes I have no idea, but all of a sudden, collectively, quite seriously the television professional in all of us took over. 'He's crossed the line again!', 'Who was in charge of that sound quality?', 'Where's the cutaway, give us the cutaway!', 'The eyelines are all over the place', 'Pan up you idiot!', 'Look at that lighting!', 'He had his socks off in the wide shot and now they're back on, don't they know anything about continuity?' And so on until, not much later, we all got bored and went out to eat. It was a pretty tatty production, all said and done.

Some years on finds me channel zapping through the ever multiplying offerings on British television. The professional programme maker is again having to watch pornography. Nothing to do with the subject matter, I am too old a horse to be fazed by bare bottoms in action and the series 'Topless Darts' strikes me as rather amusing.

The parade of flesh I can happily put up with. The parade of amateurism, ignorance and incompetence shown by some programme makers I cannot. Television, as even some company executives have admitted, is 'dumbing down'. So far only the trivia on morning and daytime television and after eleven at night is hopelessly contaminated but this is on national broadcast networks. Snapping on their heels are dozens, soon to be hundreds, of cable and satellite channels many of them competing for new levels of awfulness.

The reasons are clear. The aggregate hours to fill have increased many times faster than the money available to finance them or the skilled staff to service them. Television culture has changed and the money men are firmly in the saddle. Shareholders' profits take precedence over programme quality. New technology is used not as a means to explore new possibilities but as a golden opportunity to 'downsize', 'outsource' and 'reduce the head count'. Budgets are slashed. A half hour purely regional location programme for the BBC might have attracted a budget of £30 000 only ten years ago. Today half the amount is generous.

New national network programmes are talking of programmes at £6000 per hour! Many of those hit by the wave of redundancies in the 1990s have resurfaced in the 800 or so independent broadcast production companies which have sprung up. Technicians and designers have found homes in various facility companies.

There are still livings to be made in the old world of corporate video and the very new one of CD-ROM. But a lot of the creative side of television has shrunk to very much of a cottage industry where many little companies get by on a profitability of under 3 per cent on turnover. At the same time there has taken place an explosion in the numbers of graduates from university media studies courses, maybe this year over 30 000, many of whom hope for a job in television.

The television industry itself has been stagnant or shrinking. There are now around 28 000 workers left in the creative sectors. Hardly surprising then that training has gone to the wall. It is no longer possible to start as a humble assistant cameraman, film editor or floor manager and learn a craft from the bottom. Assistants are an endangered species. The best way to become a news cameraman in the BBC is to qualify as a despatch rider. The lucky few from the universities who get jobs may have to be willing to work initially without pay to get any kind of work experience. They will certainly be expected to become multiskilled, meaning do the jobs of office junior, producer, director, camera operator, sound recordist, presenter and scriptwriter as well as picture editor.

The one-man band all-purpose programme maker

is established on cable television and is attracting a lot of attention from the men in suits elsewhere. This is the future. The main companies may continue to make, or more likely commission, expensive drama, hard-hitting investigative journalism and ambitious documentary series. The majority of beginners though will count themselves lucky to land a short-term contract in the bargain basement of broadcasting and work under people who have scarcely more knowledge or experience than themselves.

There is no point in me, or others like me, acting like an old codger in the corner of a pub waving my walking stick at the world and lamenting the good old days to anyone daft enough to buy me a drink.

The new technology is brilliant and getting better. It is also getting cheaper and more user friendly. Maybe there will be a new generation of directors who find it quite natural to double up as camera operators or picture editors. After all there has been an honourable tradition of documentary director/ cameramen, and many famous film directors have taken hands-on command in the cutting room. Maybe old crafts will become redundant, as set design and construction is replaced by computer-generated virtual reality settings and robot cameras replace studio camera operators.

Equipment develops at a frightening pace. Sony have introduced three new different digital formats in 1997 alone! Post production and digital video effects systems are evolving at an even more spectacular rate. Go away for a long summer holiday and the very latest gear has become obsolescent; something new and wonderful has replaced it and all the talk is of something just over the horizon.

What difference ought all this make to training? 'Not a lot' is my contention. Learning to produce and direct a programme has not a lot to do with knowing which sequence to press buttons on the newest toys. A new camera might fit in the palm of the hand and be sensitive enough to work down a mine shaft. Can the operator frame and hold a good picture? Can the director set up a sequence of shots that cut together? Would a scene be improved enormously by lights and does the operator know the principles of three-point lighting, and indeed has he or she been issued with appropriate lamps? The picture editor may be able to perform an amazing number of cuts per hour but are the cuts on the right frames? Why do some work and others not? Who can recognise the difference? Does he or she know much about the principles of manipulating sound or cutting pictures to music? In brief it matters little whether the medium used is film, tape, linear, non-linear, digital, analogue, video disc or magic lantern. An effective programme is an effective programme and a lousy one is a lousy one. The difference between them is in the talent, craft, knowledge and experience of those using the equipment, not in the toys they operate.

How is the new generation to catch up on this lack of practical apprenticeship or formal training except slowly and with great difficulty? There is no question that the talent is there. What is lacking is any will to systematically nurture it.

I sincerely hope that this slim volume will help those studying media and communications at university, those trying to establish a toehold in a broadcasting or production company, or others striking out on their own as hopeful freelances. My prejudices and opinions are plain and I make no apologies for them. Television is a quirky, individualistic business and no two directors will do things the same way. None of my professional colleagues is going to agree with all of my statements or assertions. I plead in mitigation that everything is the fruit of personal practical experience and observation, particularly where anecdotal material is concerned. If subjects are skimped or ignored it is because to cover everything would be a mammoth project.

I have kept references to technology to a minimum and deliberately kept away from the details of post production. There is no point describing the procedures for a film cutting room to someone who will only work on videotape or giving advice to someone about two-machine editing of U-Matic tapes when the reader is already operating a digital non-linear system. The emphasis is on the practical craft of making programmes, the basic skills needed and the tried and tested tricks of the trade.

Where detailed production problems arise I suggest that the reader makes a cross-reference to the companion volume to this one, *The Essential Television Handbook*. I have deliberately not gone into the business of planning and executing multi camera studio programmes or outside broadcasts.

A decade or so ago a handbook like this might have taken studio direction as a starting point. Not now. This is a specialist area and increasingly so.

Whether the current generation of highly skilled studio directors will be the last time will tell. Complex studio direction needs the full back-up and technical resources of a major broadcasting company. Without this there is no way that the professional disciplines of a proper studio can survive. Studios are having a revival because they offer a cheap way of churning out material. Half a dozen quiz programmes a day are being turned around by a single director. I am assuming that the readers will at best direct the sort of studio discussion and magazine programmes produced regionally and for departments like children's programmes and educational broadcasting. They will have to work with the simplest technical and administrative support.

My own broadcasting career has spanned over thirty years, twenty five at the BBC, with the last seven of those with its Television Training Department. Since then I have worked as a freelance director and producer, and have worked around the globe as a director of Television Training International. I owe a particular debt of gratitude to my friends and colleagues at TTI and specifically to Mike Catherwood and Peter Fitton. I have known them as programme makers and training instructors at home and in far flung parts for more years than I should care to admit. To Peter Fitton I owe a particular debt of gratitude. Without his help and advice the chapter on musical performances would not have been possible.

I never cease to learn from my colleagues. That is as it should be. If I have hijacked some of their ideas I hope they take it as a compliment. Nobody ever knows everything about television. When you start this career you begin a learning curve with never an end in sight. Nobody will ever have all the answers or for that matter come across all of the questions in a single lifetime.

Television, good television, is not a career for a hack. It

needs an enthusiasm bordering on a passion. I have it and I recognize it in even the most jaundiced of my contemporaries. Like them I would like to share that enthusiasm with those now joining our business for the first time.

Peter Jarvis

My own word of warning

I am lamentably non-politically correct. I have tried wherever possible to use words like camera operator in place of cameraman and him or her instead of male pronouns alone. Where this has proved impossible or stylistically clumsy, I have retained the male form. A camera operator is not exactly the same as a cameraman; camera woman or camera person sound absurdly pedantic and I refuse to describe a human being as a camera. I have handled cameras all my life and none of them had arms and legs. I can only apologise to anybody affronted. All terms and references apply equally to both men and women. In the same vein I have played fast and loose with film and video terms. Unless the context makes it clear otherwise, I freely interchange terms like record and film, editing suite and cutting room, picture editor and film editor.

The terminology used in American English and British English is often very different, for example OB/Remote, Gallery/Control, Vision Mixer/Switcher, Presenter/Talent, Recce/Scouting and so on. With few exceptions I have kept to the British usage.

1

Television grammar

Who needs it?

Every television director does. That's who needs it. Television has a language. It is a language of pictures but also of words and sounds and music. For the most part this language derives from the cinema, which is over a century old. Cinema grammar is understood by practically the whole human race. Many of the conventions of both television and the cinema derive from photography which is nearly 200 years old, and the theatre, which is considerably older than that.

A great deal of the way we perceive the composition and lighting of pictures, and the way we read stories into them, derives from conventions established in Renaissance European painting.

John Grierson, the father of the British documentary, had the job of training directors and cameramen who were Post Office employees, often no more than messenger boys. He began by sending them to the National Gallery and National Portrait Gallery just to sit and look at the use of composition and light.

There is quite a tradition to live up to.

Television and film are narrative media. They have to be by their nature. One picture follows another at twenty four or twenty five pictures per second. Each picture adds information to the picture before and anticipates more information in the ones to come. The pace is dictated solely by the director. The reader of printed material can move at a chosen pace, slow down, read a sentence twice, skip the boring bits, refer to the footnotes, flick from script to illustrations and back again or have two publications open at once. Maybe a new generation of computer programs and cable technology will make possible this sort of intelligent random access multiple choice viewing on the television screen. But not yet.

The television world which exists now at the closing of the twentieth century, and which the readers of this book will be inhabiting for a long time to come, remains a linear narrative medium. Television producers and directors may even be heirs to the oldest profession of all, as old as the other claimant to the title. They are the storytellers and entertainers of the tribe. The first priority of storytellers and entertainers is to excite as well as communicate with their audience.

There is no point in trying to tell a story and then wilfully use a language which the audience cannot understand or a delivery which bores it into a stupor.

Television grammar is a true Esperanto. The same soap operas are comprehensible to audiences on every continent whether dubbed or undubbed, subtitled or signed manually for the impaired of hearing.

Languages do not stand still. They evolve, pick up new idioms, drop old forms and adopt new ones. Different social groups and generations may talk slightly differently to each other. There are regional differences. But the bare bones of the language, the grammar which makes communication possible at all, changes slowly or hardly at all.

Broadcast television is a popular medium. It is expensive to make and by the cruel dictates of accountancy needs to attract maximum possible viewing figures. Blockbuster costume dramas and minority series about basket weaving or Icelandic sagas share the same problem of being accessible to their widest audiences.

The content may be as populist or esoteric as you like. The images and sounds will not convey the message without a familiar language with a comprehensible grammar. Grammar can be acquired by a process of instruction and correction or through experience and emulation; generally a mixture of the two.

This assertion can be disputed. There are three arguments in favour of throwing away the whole idea of the grammar of television as an out-of-date irrelevance; rather as schools stopped teaching Latin. They run:

1   There is a youth (yoof) generation brought up on the anarchic visual language of pop videos and commercials, who routinely channel-zap between ever-increasing numbers of transmissions and whose recreation is computer games. This audience exists bombarded by a cacophony of amplified music and a blitz of images which it is capable of deciphering without help from anyone else. Its attention

span may be measured in seconds, not hours or minutes. Every image ought to be novel, spectacular and arresting. There is no time or need for pedantic rules.

2   The mystery has gone out of the craft. Everyone with a few hundred pounds can buy technical equipment almost as good as that used by broadcasters. Families have domestic video equipment as well as snapshot cameras. They are happy with what was once unacceptably amateur. Why complain about unsteady pans and zooms, jump cuts in vision or weird camera angles? Nobody is confused any more. Everyone understands the technology and how to operate it and the professionally trained elite are becoming irrelevant anachronisms. Television is thoroughly democratic at last.

3   Television grammar is just a boring way for the old guard to stifle originality and creativity. Television is an art form. Artists have proved repeatedly that they can tear up the rule books and create new languages from scratch. Learning about yesterday's television grammar is an academic irrelevance holding the medium from its artistic potential.

There are no absolute answers to these assertions. This book does though hope to demolish them. All three propositions come to much the same thing. From now on with broadcast television, anything goes. This is all one with the fashionable school of English criticism that sees Shakespeare and Mills and Boon romances as having equal value. It just depends on what the reader feels like at the time.

My rebuttal is as follows:

1   Youth generations are short lived and spend a great deal of time reinventing the wheel. Each new generation thinks that it is unique and more innovative than every one before. Each in turn becomes exasperated by the callow pretensions of the next cohort treading at its heels. The young are always quick to pick up on new technological developments and claim them for their own. They don't have the burden of having to unlearn old habits. An effortless familiarity with computers is an obvious generation difference of the present era.

There is a desperation about the courting of successive yoof generations by television companies. The main proponents have tended to be middle-aged ladies and

3

gentlemen in unsuitable clothes. This is nothing new, it has been going on ever since the first pop music programmes of the 1950s. It has never fully succeeded. Youth is not yoof. It comprises young coarse fishermen, ballroom dancers, computer freaks, car obsessives, synchronized swimmers, pigeon fanciers and an awful lot of people just worried about passing their exams. The anticipated audience figures never quite materialize. Most young people from their early teens to their early twenties have got better, more amusing and important things to do than be condescended to by television producers.

Genuine youth styles appear unannounced leaving broadcasters behind with yesterday's fads. Making presenters imitate an inarticulate mumble, use the latest slang (nothing dates faster), having every camera shot at a whacky angle and covering edits with explosive video effects and crashing bars of rock music does not create an innovative style. It insults its target audience.

There has been a dynamic input from pop music videos. Directors have been able to experiment with all manner of new techniques. They have been a cradle of innovation for digital video effects. They have introduced computer imagery to mainstream television grammar. Remember though the reason why pop music directors have such licence is because most videos are all form and very little substance: 'All sound and fury signifying nothing', to quote an earlier author, or, as more popularly expressed, 'nice video, pity about the song'.

The biggest yoof audience-pullers in fact seem to be mainstream programmes like soap operas which follow the narrative grammar and dramatic conventions meticulously. Everyone has to grow up eventually. Except perhaps the people who make yoof programmes.

2 The home video argument has proved very attractive to cost-conscious programme executives. Access to good amateur equipment has given rise to an innovative and often very revealing 'video diary' format. It can open options to travel programmes which get holidaymakers to shoot their own videos so saving a fortune in travel and accommodation for researchers and camera crews. Technical standards used to be a bar to transmission

of amateur stuff on broadcast channels but this is decreasingly so.

There are drama directors who wilfully imitate the style of the home video under the impression that this imparts a sort of specious integrity to the work. They keep their cameras constantly ducking and diving, panning and zooming. What this does to the viewer has been described by one distinguished reviewer as feeling like being on a switchback ride, clutching the sides of the armchair whilst the cameraman behaves like an alcoholic bungee jumper.

The difference between a typical home video and a professionally directed story remains profound even if sometimes it can be a breath of fresh air to watch an inspired though technically primitive item. The main distinguishing feature of home videos is that they are by their nature self-indulgent. They do not aspire to communicate any message or grip an otherwise disinterested audience. Most are probably watched once or twice only. Most are excruciatingly tedious to anyone apart from the perpetrators and their immediate circle. Audience figures consistently infer that the majority of viewers will always opt for a well-crafted and grammatically sound piece of work. Doubters need only to look where the real money is found, in cinema feature films, popular television drama and live action commercials. They follow the universal grammatical rules and conventions.

3   Film and video have attracted the attention of creative individuals from their earliest days. The surrealists of the 1920s and the video artists of today share a fascination with manipulating moving images. The real explosion in innovation has been in digital effects and graphics. There has always been an important minority art cinema. Broadcast television has tended to remain conservative, as has most of commercial cinema. The advent of hundreds of cable and satellite channels may change all this. There may become available facilities for the broadcast of purely experimental work to minuscule audiences of aficionados. This book does not dismiss the abstract and the innovative, or denigrate those who would develop television as a fine art form. It is simply written

with those in mind who will accept that directing broadcast television involves knowing a set of basic practical crafts based on tried and tested skills.

It is worth pointing out to sceptics that the work of some of the most innovative British directors of recent years, like Peter Greenaway and Derek Jarman, observe the conventions of traditional grammar in their picture composition, lighting and editing. They too are in the business of telling stories.

Breaking the rules, or at least playing fast and loose with conventions, can be liberating. It is sometimes necessary if television programmes are not to be stuck forever in an ever-deepening rut. Here is a simple plea to the newcomer. Before trying new ways learn what the old rules are, and why they have been so universally adopted. Television grammar is rooted in universal human psychology and social responses. We respond to sounds and images less because of conditioning by television itself but because well-made television mirrors the way we constantly interpret the everyday world without the benefit of a camera lens.

Here endeth the lesson. Asking not just what to do and how to do it, but why it ought to be done at all is the starting point of the director's craft.

Shot sizes

Television is a collaborative craft. Even the all-singing, all-dancing one-man or one-woman multiskilled video journalist has colleagues. In order to communicate quickly and clearly a shorthand jargon has developed. The descriptions of shot sizes is the case in point.

There are standard terms for describing pictures. Panoramic views are loosely defined as Wide Shots or Wide Angles, referring to the use of a wide angle of view. Closer pictures of details from the same camera position are referred to as Tight Shots. If a wide shot serves the purpose of establishing the geographical setting for a story, the director might ask for a GV, short for a General View. Camera operators will instantly understand these terms without the need for more precise definition. For example, 'Give me a wide angle of the garden and then tight shots of the two greenhouses'.

When it comes to pictures of human beings the language is

far more precise. It would be a waste of time for a director to try to describe a required shot in standard English sentences such as 'Could we have a shot showing more of her hair and I'd like to see her pearl necklace. No, not so much as that. I don't want to see her hands. . .' or 'I wonder if you could make him look a bit like that lovely shot in Citizen Kane, you know the big one where the camera sort of looks up Orson Welles' nose. . .'

It is more precise and less effort to say 'Show me a mid-shot' or 'a low-angle mid close-up'.

For a lot of the time television cameras are pointed at people, and in particular at people's faces. How those people and faces are shown is the decision of the director. The same performer can be shown as a distant dot on the horizon or be shot so close that the eyes and mouth fill the screen. The common shot sizes and description are:

- the very long shot (VLS)
- the long shot (LS)
- the mid-shot (MS)
- the mid close-up (MCU)
- the close-up (CU)
- the big close-up (BCU)

Studio directors in particular us the abbreviations MS, MCU, etc. all the time. This is the shorthand way they always appear on scripts. There is not time in the control gallery to use complete terms.

The location director may have greater opportunity to work out creative compositions but will still avoid a lot of grief by communicating with a technical crew using familiar standard shot descriptions.

Choosing a shot size should *never* be done at random, or because a director feels bored and would like to see something a bit different. Shot sizes should not just happen because the director or journalist in charge has never given the matter a moment's thought and left everything to a camera operator.

Every picture tells a story. The way something as familiar as a human face is framed on the television screen adds or subtracts information and tells the viewer something new about the subject. There is no escaping the fact that to set up a camera with a particular shot is to make an editorial comment as surely as by writing a sentence of commentary. The basic shot sizes have both technical uses for the director and convey straightforward psychological messages to the viewers.

Figure 1.1

The very long shot

The VLS (Figure 1.1) belongs on location programmes to establish a character in a landscape. It is most useful for the cinema where screen size is the advantage. Its limitation for television appears when the presenter or interviewer starts to speak. Whether the performer is talking on a radio microphone, or the shot is to be included as a cutaway, the perspective of the sound will be close up, as though the speaker was standing alongside the viewer. The convention using close-up sound with distant images is well established in drama. Factual programmes can show the limitations. It can be arresting to start a story with a panoramic shot of a gasometer crowned by a reporter in VLS but the shot becomes very uneasy if held for more than few seconds. The figure is too far for lip movements or facial expression to be seen. When someone starts talking to us we have a natural urge to want to see who it is. We need to cut in to a closer shot. The mismatch of sound and picture can become irksome. From such a distance someone would need to shout or use a loud hailer to address us. Once the relevance of the location has been understood the shot has outstayed its welcome.

The long shot

An LS (Figure 1.2) portrays the whole body from head to feet. The technical use of the LS is to establish the geographical

Figure 1.2

context of the performer without losing interest in him or her. It is a good shot for establishing a studio with a crowded set, such as a popular science magazine or a music show with numerous set-ups and a boisterous audience. This is one shot that often needs a bit of additional direction. At its longest the shot may be distant enough for lip reading to be impossible and so can be used as an opening shot with overlaid sound. The director needs to decide whether synchronous lip movements are needed or not.

On location there may be practical problems. The wider the angle of view the greater the risk of something distracting cropping up in the background. This might be the ever-lurking teenage lout waving at the viewer or something as easy to miss as a bright red car passing through shot. The human eye is perversely prone to distraction and bright colours or sudden movement can easily escape the notice of a director and a camera operator. A long shot on a narrow angle of view increases the distance between the camera and the subject. This in turn increases the risk of something intruding in the foreground and also can lead to sound difficulties. The long shot is an ideal one for documentary style programmes where a presenter acts as a guide; for example, a naturalist in a jungle or an art critic in a gallery. In this context the LS is a natural choice. It is the way we would see someone leading a party around a stately home or would watch the demonstration of a piece of large equipment. Performer and location are given a shared importance in the picture. To add extra interest directors often choose to have their performers in long shot walking towards or past the camera whilst speaking. If the cameras can simultaneously pan with the walk the effect will be even better. In the context of a crowded refugee camp or abandoned town the effect can be stunningly effective as each step will reveal fresh information to the viewer. Unfortunately the walkie-talkie LS can be a mere cliché attempt to pep up dreary material. Yoof presenters are particularly afflicted by this perpetual motion. Hyperactive reporters who are perpetually on the move for no good reason are likely to infuriate rather than impress. The reason why the viewer wants to cry out 'stand still will you' is rooted in everyday psychology. We willingly follow a guide explaining to us new things. We avoid lunatics who wander about talking loudly to themselves.

The mid-shot

The MS (Figure 1.3) is one of the commonest framings for seated interviews. It shows the whole trunk together with the arms and hands of the subject. It enables the viewer to observe the expression in the eyes, the physical body language and the dress style. It is the commonest composition for portrait painters. It would be an ideal composition for television were it not for the unalterable geometry of the standard screen. A

Figure 1.3

photographer will rotate the camera through 90° to change the picture composition from the normal 'landscape' format to the 'portrait' format. To achieve the same result on television we would have to warn viewers to stand their set on end.

The mid-shot on television reveals a deal of background information. This can be all for the good particularly at the beginning of studio interviews where the viewer needs to be reminded of the geography of the setting and where there may be a need to show a programme logo. The MS is also the shot of choice if there is the intention of superimposing name captions over the lower third of the screen. Any closer shot risks the printed words obscuring part of the face. Psychologically it is the way we feel easiest looking at strangers. Close enough to be able to give attention, interested but not intimate. It is a favourite framing for news readers.

There is a variation often preferred by location reporters, the medium long shot (MLS), known as the American shot in most European languages. The standing subject here is framed wider than the MS and cut off at around knee level. It is a compromise shot often imposed by the problems of the location. Many directors and cameramen find it ugly.

> **Helpful hint**
> If location problems mean that the best useful shots are not beautiful there is an easy test to see whether they will be acceptable and, most important, they will cut with other shots in the same sequence. Whether the shot is an LS or BCU or anything in between, make sure that the eyes are framed on a line exactly two thirds up the screen and the bridge of the nose is framed at the centre. The shots will now probably work even with a jump cut between an LS and an MCU.

The mid close-up

The MCU (Figure 1.4) is the all-purpose workhorse shot of the television screen. On the standard screen it is the most flattering portrait format and is the equivalent of the composition of the bust favoured in classical portrait sculpture. The MCU shows complete head and shoulders but excludes all but a hint of background. The viewer concentrates on the all-important facial expression but has extra information from shoulder movements

Figure 1.4

and dress. The shot is intimate but not obtrusive. It is easy to frame and hold in focus and is wide enough to cope with unexpected head and shoulder movements without the subject ducking out of the frame. It can be discreetly widened to accommodate hand gestures. Many short interviews can be conducted almost entirely using MCUs. It is the framing we adopt naturally when engaged in serious conversation.

A point for directors to watch though is although the MCU is the commonest standard shot in standard television, cameramen from news departments often describe it simply as a close-up. The reason is that in news there is rarely any use for closer shots.

The close-up

This is the most powerful of the normal close shots and because of that it has to be treated with caution. This shot fills the frame with the human face from the neck to the top of the hair. In drama the CU (Figure 1.5) is used to heighten tension or show mounting passions. In factual programmes and interviews it is appropriate for the most intimate of subjects or the most emotionally personal of recollections. In interviews it is the shot to hold in reserve for the moment when the challenging question is anticipated:

> 'So have you accepted bribes, yes or no?'

Figure 1.5

or 'What was your first reaction when the disease was
diagnosed?'

Even if the words fail to come the eyes will speak volumes.
It is not a shot to waste on 'Will you show us how to fry the
mushrooms?' or 'What are your fashion tips for the coming
season?' Presenters or reporters should not appear in close-
up except for the rarest dramatic revelations or commentary
punch lines. If a close-up is held on the screen too long and
the verbal content is banal the picture soon loses its power. Far
from concentrating the attention of the viewer it will wander
off to consider the crows' feet around the eyes or the quality of
the dentistry on show.

Again these rules are dictated by common sense. An intimate
shot can also be an embarrassing one. Observe any group of
strangers in a crowded lift or underground train. They are
forced into an intimacy where they are obliged to look at each
other in CUs. They will do anything possible to alter their body
and head positions to avoid each other's gaze. Give them
more space so that they can stand back just far enough to
regard each other in mid-shot and they immediately become
relaxed. At a social gathering the only people who choose to
talk at close-up distance are probably conspiring or starting a
love affair.

Figure 1.6

The big close-up

This is the most intimate of all. The face is reduced to eyes, nose and mouth. There are only two common social circumstances when people have their faces so close and the end results will be either a passionate kiss or a punch on the nose.

Technically the shot creates problems for the camera. BCUs (Figure 1.6) and CUs involve using the narrow end of the zoom lens and if the head moves even slightly backwards or forwards it can dip in and out of focus. If, as happens more often, the head bobs from side to side, part or all of the face vanishes out of the side of the frame before the camera operator has a chance to adjust the composition. The BCU risks being overwhelming and melodramatic. The only person to come so close in real life is the party drunk who pins his victim up against the wall or the interrogator intimidating his victim. Like some other intimate situations CUs and BCUs are easier to get into than to get out of.

Once the director has heightened the mood to the point of arriving at BCUs there is really nowhere else to go. Visually the shots have reached the point of melodrama. If the interest of the piece continues to mount there is no more exciting framing to match. If the subject matter ceases to justify the framing the subsequent shots will have to be widened out to MCUs and MSs which can imply to the viewer that the item is coming to an end or the director is losing interest. The safest place for the close-ups is as a climax to a dramatic sequence immediately before a cut to a different scene. Unfortunately they have also been used as a conventional way in American soaps to cue a commercial break.

Closer my Lord to Thee

Finally there appear from time to time BCUs so close that they present a physical intimacy unattainable even by lovers and familiar only to dentists and ear, nose and throat consultants. Shots filling the screen entirely with teeth and lips or eyes and nostrils have perhaps some use in feature films, e.g. a cutaway of a teardrop forming, or sweat on the lip of a bomber at the last second of a countdown. Spaghetti Westerns in the 1970s made a cliché of successively closer shots in Main Street gun duels. Then, Spaghetti Westerns were mostly spoofs.

From 1997 these huge anatomical shots have started to crop up in television programmes as various as a lecture series on economics and party political broadcasts.

The offence has been compounded by shooting them in profile. The impression is boredom with the subject matter, contempt for the attention span of the viewer and wilful ignorance by the director who should not be allowed out to play again without a promise to stop showing off.

Wide screen

Wide screen television has been around since the early 1980s and anticipated as the emerging screen format annually since then. There has been constantly changing technology and an inability to agree a common international standard for wide screen, and high definition TV which goes with it. There are also high level international political and commercial battles. No one company or country wants a rival to scoop the pool by dominating the next generation of television for the whole world. Wide screen television has been a long time a-coming. Nonetheless for some time many directors have chosen to shoot prestigious dramas and documentaries on Super 16 wide screen film which has a 16:9 ratio, and the newest video cameras have the facility to switch between this and the old 4:3 ratio.

Wide screen domestic sets can be bought but most wide screen productions are watched on the old almost square screens. Then either part of the picture at the sides of the screen has to be sacrificed or the image must be letter boxed to include both sides but leaving a part of the screen area as black bands top and bottom. When wide screen high definition does finally arrive, possibly with far larger screen sizes, some of the conventions about television shot composition may have to be rewritten. MCUs will no longer exclude most background and a centre framing may no longer be the ideal. Profile two-shots may become attractive possibilities. Mid-shots can be attractively framed off-centre though the rule for positioning the eyes exactly two-thirds up the screen still generally applies.

A lot more attention has to be paid to lighting and design and selecting location settings. But the viewer will still have to be provided with shots which are comfortable to watch. Psychological motivations for selecting one shot over another will remain. If traditional visual grammar holds good for wide screen cinema there is no reason for it to be abandoned for a new generation of television sets.

Camera angles

Choosing the right shot sizes and cutting them in an appropriate sequence is part of the story. Placing them in the right relationship to the eyeline of the subject is another. The size of shot tells the viewer about the geography of the studio set or the location, the gravity of the content and the intimacy of the subject matter. Lens angles reveal the nature of the relationship of performers one to another. Seemingly every human language has turns of phrase which refer to looking up to superior beings and looking down at inferior ones. Emperors are raised on thrones, subjects bow or prostrate themselves.

Barons ate at high tables, underlings sat below the salt. The rich are high and mighty and upper class, the lower classes exist below stairs and are probably downcast. Underlings slaving for overseers want to get above their position and get a place at the top. The list is endless. The easiest way to show the dominance of one character over another is to shoot the dominant one looking down towards the lens and the submissive one from a lower position looking up. It is universal and instantly recognized body language (Figures 1.7 and 1.8).

Figure 1.7

Figure 1.8

Drama directors use this simple observation in everything from police interrogation scenes to light situation comedy. The quickest way to signpost a reversal of roles is for one character to sit and the other to rise. Add these angles to unequal shot sizes which give the dominant character a tighter more powerful framing than the weaker one and the visual message is complete. Words are unnecessary. In factual programmes directors mostly try to maintain absolutely straight eyelines. The lens ought to be precisely level with the eyes of the subject so that the image will be neutral.

When this is not the case it is generally the result of the inexperience of the director and the laziness of an operator who fails to adjust tripod height between set-ups. This can be more serious than a matter of peculiar looking pictures. Politicians in particular are taught about television grammar and they will automatically assume intent. So by all means use varying lens heights to give style to a story but never forget that every non-standard shot is making an editorial comment.

Shooting a captain of industry from a low angle against a background of towering skyscrapers may give an impression of enormous power and personal charisma. This is in fact the way captains of industry love to be photographed for publication in their own management magazines. This can risk misjudging the natural reactions of an ordinary viewer. The captain of industry might love the idea of looking down from a position of power, other industrialists may love to identify with such images. Other people may resent being looked down on. If the rest of the story fails to endorse the gigantic importance of the man so portrayed the picture takes on another meaning. One man's heroic leader becomes another man's posturing ass. If this is the impression the director wishes to convey, the low-angle interview shot is one way to achieve it without the slightest recourse to defamatory words. Nobody yet has been sued for defamation by camera angle (accompanying background music is another case, however).

When high and low angles are to be intercut they have to match. The shot looking down must be the exact reverse angle of the shot looking up. In all cases the eyeline has to be towards the lens. The ugliest of all compromises is where the camera lens is higher or lower than the eyes of a subject who continues to speak directly ahead to a second party. In a drama about a political rally this can be a very dramatic device. The eyeline is that of someone at the front of the crowd peering up at the orator. In a standard television factual programme the result of unmatched lens heights and eyelines just reveals dreadful camerawork.

Lens angles

The angle of position of the camera to the subject must not be confused with the angle of view of the lens. This is a third vital consideration to understand when framing a shot. Film cinematographers are accustomed to choosing between a wide range of different fixed angle lenses all of which have different characteristics and subtly influence how each shot looks. Today most video cameras are used with a single zoom lens, although some allow for an interchangeable wide-angle zoom alternative. There are also usually electronic image multipliers and macro facilities built into video cameras.

A word of warning

The zoom is not a toy to enable the camera operator to yank the image back and forth in vision. It was designed to offer an infinite choice of fixed angle lenses attainable through a single combination of glass and metal. A zoom in vision is not something we can experience through the human eye or brain. Eyes do not zoom. An emphatic zoom in vision is a trick visual effect and no more. The zoom must not be treated as a facility which enables a camera operator to get the same size framing from almost any position without having to take the trouble to move the tripod from A to B. Used properly the zoom lens offers almost infinite flexibility. Used randomly it results in sloppy camera work and insoluble editing problems.

There are pleasing shots and there are ugly shots. But there are no universally right or wrong shots, only shots which are right or wrong for their context. The key is to understand how a choice of a lens angle may be defined by the context of a scene. Take, for example, a seated mid-shot of a man in a park. It is clear that much the same framing can be achieved whether the camera tripod is standing three feet or thirty feet away from the subject. All the operator apparently has to do is zoom in or out. From a near camera position the lens will be opened out to a wide angle for an MS, from a distant position the operator will have to zoom in to a very narrow angle. Both camera positions can offer the director what can fairly be described as mid-shots of the subject. Unfortunately these two mid-shots will be completely unalike.

First, the wider the angle of the lens and the closer the camera is to the subject the greater will be the depth of field. In other words the more of the background and most of the foreground will be seen in sharp focus. The narrower the angle of view and the further away the camera is from the subject the shallower will be the depth of field; any foreground and background will become progressively out of focus. The less light there is on the scene the more emphatic this effect will become. At a point the camera may even have trouble keeping all features on the face in sharp focus.

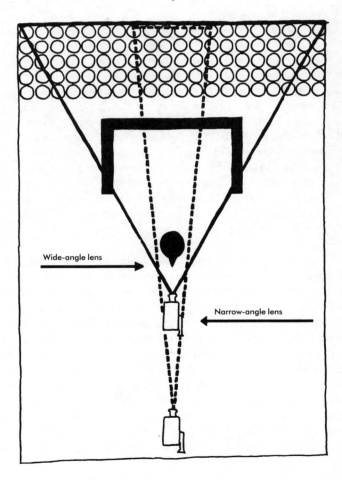

Figure 1.9

Second, the wider the angle of view the wider will appear the background perspective. For example, if our MS subject is standing by the goalmouth in a football stadium and the camera is close up using a wide-angle lens the whole stadium (Figure 1.9) will be in shot as a clearly focused background. Conversely the narrower the angle of view the narrower will be the background in vision. Only a small section of seating will be discernible. Beyond a certain point this becomes irrelevant because such background as there is will be reduced to an out-of-focus blur. The director must make a conscious decision. Is it important to see the whole stadium? If the story is about safety and seating, then it probably is. If the story is about match rigging it probably isn't. If the empty seats tell a tale of falling attendances, they are essential. If there is random cleaning or maintenance work going on while the story is about bribery, they will just distract.

A very narrow angle of the reporter might be dramatically arresting but rather negate the purpose of being on the pitch in the first place. Placing the camera several yards back might offer the compromise; an MS of the presenter with a clearly focused goal post and net in the background to establish the location but not much else to distract the eye.

Third, the closer the camera to the subject and the wider the angle of view the greater will appear the distortion of the image. The perspective can become so extreme that anything in the immediate foreground appears huge. Someone looking straight at camera will be distorted. Noses will be wider and fatter than normal, ears will recede and knees in the foreground will look elephantine. On very wide angles any vertical lines like the edges of buildings or lamp-posts will seem to curve. The overall effect can become like looking at a scene in the back of a spoon. The widest of wide angles is the fish eye lens. Narrow angles are more flattering. Fashion photographers always shoot their models on moderately long lenses even for big close-up shots.

Fourth, the further away the camera and the narrower the angle of view the greater will be the difficulty of holding a steady shot. There is no point in trying narrow-angle shots with a hand-held camera. At the narrowest end of the zoom even the breathing of the operator or a slight gust of wind can emphasize camera shake. Suspension bridges can seem to bounce like trampolines. Conversely, on the wide angle any camera shake is scarcely noticed. The latest cameras have image stabilizing systems but they are unlikely to cope with very distant hand-held shots and are no help with light problems.

The closer the camera and the wider the angle of view the greater the distance apart foreground objects may seem to be. This is a crucial point to consider when lining up two shots for interviews. It may be helpful for sound purposes and enable the operator to shoot an interview on a hand-held camera but a deep two-shot on a wide-angle lens will portray the foreground figure as huge and overwhelming whilst the further one will appear shrunken and unnaturally distant. Any object between them, like a table, will emphasize this distancing. In brief the shot is ugly.

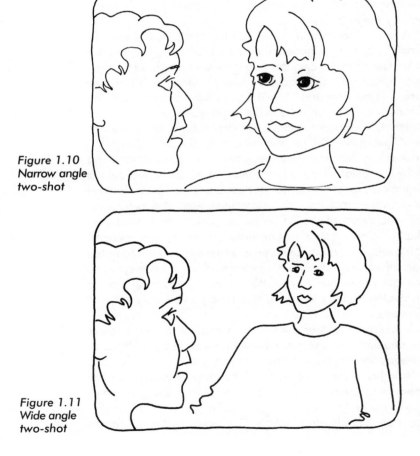

Figure 1.10
Narrow angle
two-shot

Figure 1.11
Wide angle
two-shot

The further away the camera and the narrower the lens angle the more the distance between the two subjects will appear compressed. In a very narrow-angle two-shot (Figure 1.10) the body sizes of both characters will appear almost equal. They will seem almost nose to nose. In studio interviews it is a valuable trick to heighten a sense of confrontation by pulling back two cameras as far as possible and shooting tight two-shots on narrow lens angles. The space between the two is compressed and an impression of confrontation is heightened. In the studio camera shake is not a problem. The studio has the advantage of perfectly controllable lighting and plenty of it. A practical limitation on location will be lighting ar.d resulting focus problems.

Shots from contrasting angles of view do not cut together. It is no good shooting the close-ups of an interviewee on a narrow-angle lens with the camera twelve metres distant but then recording the two-shots and reverse-angle questions on wide angles with the camera close up. The two will not cut. Even with an interview limited to two intercut MCUs the camera positions and angles of view should match, otherwise the weird impression can be given of the backgrounds advancing and retreating between shots. The studio director can match up the shots on the monitor screens before starting. The location director has to use wits and observation. The operator who appears never to adjust the tripod between shots and not match camera distances, or the one who seems to leap about all over the place between set-ups with a hand-held camera, needs to be asked for an explanation.

If this still sounds complex and esoteric the answer is to suck it and see. It is only basic photography. A stills camera with a good zoom or a single lens reflex camera with interchangeable wide-angle and telephoto lenses will illustrate the point as well as a video camera. Go out and experiment.

There are all sorts of other possibilities and problems which arise the moment that either the camera or the performers are directed to move about in vision. This takes us forward to the challenges of documentary and drama and later chapters.

To recapitulate, even when directing the simplest shot the essential considerations are:

- Which shot sizes are needed?
- What lens heights and eyelines are required?

- What is the most desirable camera position?
- Which is the most appropriate lens angle?
- How effectively will the shots cut together?

If those questions can be answered the director is ready to take on the commonest of television formats, the interview.

2

It's only an interview

See whether the following script seems familiar. The formula is regularly employed on any subject from an outbreak of bubonic plague to a report about tap dancing seagulls and is the trademark of all and any of the dozens of nearly identical topical news and current affairs magazine programmes that go out daily.

Newsreader in vision. Adopting grim or quizzical tone as appropriate.

Feelings ran high at Cardiff Docks...

Newsreader out of vision. Random cutaway shots illustrating story. Plague victims, ambulances, musical wildfowl.

Newsreader in vision.

From Cardiff Joe Hack reports.

Hack in vision. Standing next to sign saying Cardiff Docks. Wipe in name caption with programme logo Joe Hack Reporting.

In Cardiff tonight feelings...

Hack out of vision Cutaway man striding awkwardly through shot or shuffling papers at a desk looking left to right.

...Councillor Evan Evans explains.

Evan Evans in chair, close-up looking right to left. Hack out of vision. Jump cut to close-up Evan Evans in mid-sentence head at different angle. Name caption Cllr. Evan Evans.

...so how did you feel when you heard that...?
Devastated completely devastated, it was a complete...

Jump cut to Evans in middle of different sentence.	*...urgent action by Government.*
Hack in vision.	*...one thing remains certain...* Joe Hack, Cardiff, Wales.

This format of intro-cutaways-interview-cutaways-outro has become so entrenched in some TV reporters' minds that anyone who suggests alternative approaches is regarded almost as speaking in tongues.

An interview looks an easy option. The interviewee can be allowed to ramble on in expectation of a relevant 'sound bite'. If he or she provides nothing of the sort there is always the hope that a few phrases can be spliced together out of context to make something that sounds intelligible. The camera operator, if there is one, bangs off some general cutaway shots whilst the journalist writes some words for the camera. The whole package is handed to a picture editor to be cut long or short as time allows. The pictures may have only a remote relationship to the scripted commentary. They may not cut together coherently. If they do it will be regarded as fortuitous. In a journalist-dominated programme words can be all that count. An obsession with 'hold the front page' immediacy compounds the problem. Most editors seem to prefer a garbled half intelligible ill cut snippet that gets on air 15 minutes earlier than a rival magazine to a sensibly constructed story appearing a short time later. It never occurs that the only places in the world where half a dozen rival services are constantly monitored are television newsrooms. Unless the subject is an ongoing siege, disaster or incoming election results the normal viewers do not give a damn.

Curiously the last thing often considered is whether the interviewee has anything worthwhile to say, or is capable of expressing it, or even is allowed enough air-time to express a coherent viewpoint. The interview is taken too often as an effortless way to turn pigs' ears into silk purses. Unfortunately the number of incomprehensible interview-based reports on air indicate that a pig's ear is a pig's ear is a pig's ear.

Interviews come in all forms and lengths, live and edited, on location and in studio, on outside broadcasts and through satellite links. They are popular with both programme makers and programme accountants. They are easy to set up and fill the maximum transmission time at the lowest possible cost. Interviews with discussion programmes, proliferate in the wastelands of daytime television and provide the backbone of low budget cable productions.

Talk is cheap

Many creative programme makers react violently against the abuse of interviews. They maintain rightly that television is all about telling stories with moving pictures. For them the formal interview is a sell out. Terms like 'television for the blind' and 'radio with pictures' are used. This is a pity. 'Talking heads' do not justify their bad reputation. The human face provides a fascinating, informative picture. A tale well told, or emotion expressed and an argument sincerely put often have no need of cutaways and pictorial interruptions.

An intelligently conducted interview allows the viewer to eavesdrop on a conversation, engage in a debate and witness at first hand the passions of others. The shifty eyes, the vacuous grin, the angry glare and the panic stricken hesitation help us to draw conclusions. Words alone may make it easy to concentrate on the logic of an argument. This is a great strength of radio. But words alone may conceal personality. In daily life we condition our judgements as much by body language as by words. It is a universal human trait to make conclusions about someone on the basis of facial expression, bodily appearance, clothing and gesture. This may not be fair and is never politically correct but it is patently so. Consider television drama. How much screen time is occupied by conversations or confrontations intercut between two or three characters? The commonest dramatic situations on television are in effect scripted interviews. Conversely successful interviews take on all the characteristics of drama.

As there is a difference between interviewing for radio and for television there is a difference between interviewing for television and for print. Because so many interviewers and their editors have had a print journalism training this is often overlooked. The banality of so many topical reports is the result of trying to impose newspaper values on a very different medium. By understanding and applying simple television techniques a potentially dreary set of questions and answers can be used as creatively as any other programme format.

Casting the interviewee

There may not always be a choice. A director/reporter cannot always pick and choose in matters like the survivor of a disaster or the leader of a political faction. But in many cases choices do exist. Most people are capable of giving some sort of interview but the best one to do the job is not always the first or the most obvious available. As far as circumstances allow interviewees ought to be selected with the care that an entertainment director casts performers.

Beware of official nominees

The professional spokesperson is rarely worth an interview. The menace of the sound bite descended on television during the 1990s when politicians found that they and their 'spin doctors' could reliably exploit the laziness of broadcast journalists by feeding them short and pithy quotes which required no editing. Far better to find contributors with something personal and original to say. Official statements and press releases are best used as source material for properly written commentary.

Beware of going to the top

The curse of corporate videos has always been the assumption that the man wearing the most important suit, the managing director or the chairman, must always be first choice. The results rarely do anyone any favours. The top man may be a pompous ass. He may be unable to grasp the difference between presenting a company report and giving an unscripted interview. Fear of losing face in front of colleagues may result in a demand for prepared questions and scripted answers. As bad is the interviewee who insists on appearing even though he or she has more important things in the diary and will only spare a few minutes. Those new to television always underestimate how long everything takes.

Do your own research

For a thirty minute profile the interviewer will need to have devoted time to reading up both the subject and what is known personally about the interviewee. If a researcher is involved there must be time for a good clear briefing. It is horribly embarrassing to watch a studio interview in which the host blunders relentlessly through a set of prepared questions regardless of the answers. Any kind of interview will fall apart if the guest realizes that the interviewer doesn't know what he or she is talking about.

Be aware of the programme audience

An interview has to be pitched at a level appropriate to the programme and the target audience. A guest cannot be expected to know what the director has in mind. If the research has been good there should be a range of supplementary and alternative questions at hand to winkle out the sort of responses which are required. Experts and academics often pitch their answers at a level too rarefied for easy comprehension or try to qualify even simple statements. Do not worry about acting a little dim by following complex answers by a supplementary question along the lines:

> 'Fascinating, but I'm not sure I've completely followed the bit about X. Could you explain it to me more simply?'

The interviewee might of course start by saying:

> 'Well as I just told you...'

but you stand a good chance of getting a usable short version of what has gone before without having to stop shooting to conduct a conference.

Talk it through

Except in some kinds of political interrogation where the interview becomes a debate, the guest is the person who counts. The journalist is no more than a facilitator. Before the camera turns you should always talk through the line of questioning, suggest which topics or anecdotes might be helpful, and let the guest know as far as possible the nature of the programme, the context in which the interview may be used and how long the edited version, or the studio slot, is likely to be. This will allow both participants to size each other up. Relaxed replies or more spontaneous verbal sparring can result. An informal chat whilst the crew are setting up lights and microphones quite often reveals unexpected lines of questioning. Above all this is the time to spot and head off likely digressions and irrelevancies. 'That's fascinating, professor, I didn't know that, but I don't think we'll have time. I wonder if we could go straight to your story about the laboratory cat?' One risk is that an interviewee might smell a rat and try to stake out no-go areas. It is for the skilled interviewer and the director to decide whether these matter or whether a clever restructuring can approach the same subject matter in a different way. Surprisingly few guests clam up or walk off the set once an interview is under way.

Do not rehearse

An interview lacking spontaneity it not worth having. The unpredictable should be expected even within the constraints of a live studio programme. Recorded location interviews always have an element of unpredictability though they have the advantage that the irrelevant can be cut out later and botched answers retaken. Never rehearse the actual questions and answers even if the camera operator or sound recordist asks for a trial run for technical reasons. Better to fall back on the old cliché question, 'What did you have for breakfast?' Otherwise there is the likelihood that the guest will use up the best stories in rehearsal and react as if certain answers had already been recorded.

Carefully memorized replies do not make for successful interviews. At worst the guests can even forget that they are supposed to be talking to the interviewer and start addressing the camera and the viewers directly. It is for such reasons both party political broadcasts and sycophantic showbiz celebrity interviews are often so toe-curlingly awful. Do everything possible to prevent guests using prepared notes or reference material when they are on camera. If they do not drop them half way through the interview their eyes will be perpetually flickering up and down. An interview will become impossible if a nervous guest starts referring to obscure facts and figures or quoting page numbers of a document which the viewer cannot see. Notes are the comfort blanket of the terrified. Disregard any tantrums and physically take them away before the camera turns over. The guest will come over much better as a result.

Don't bully

All location single camera interviews and many recorded studio ones are shot with editing in mind. As editing regularly takes at least twice the time as shooting, the skilful director/reporter structures the interview to minimize the time in the edit suite. This can though be taken to extremes. The insecure interviewee may plead for time to rehearse questions and answers. There is also a type of journalist who bludgeons a contributor into giving a prescribed wording at a precise duration and will submit the victim to endless retakes in order to achieve this end. On one national weekend political series the editor ordained that commentary scripts, including exact interview questions and answers, were to be submitted before reporters or camera crews ever went out. No matter that on location the guest had found something more interesting to say, or did not fully agree with the opinion he was supposed to express. The end result looked and sounded like a conference of speak-your-weight machines in suits, though the transcripts read wonderfully on paper. (This was sadly irrelevant to the career of the said editor who rose to the pinnacle of British television management.)

Structure the interview

If you are going for a single subject there is probably no need for more than three main questions. Do not start by asking a lot of barely relevant biographical details or background issues. It is a complete waste of everyone's time. Attention will wander and the guest will likely forget which subject areas or anecdotes were suggested at the earlier discussion. Get to the subject as fast as possible and stick to it. Even before post production the interview ought to have a discernible structure. The cameraman needs to know when to anticipate shifts of emphasis or subject matter and what framing or shot changes are required. Any surprise questions should be built up to carefully and anticipated by everyone (except the interviewee).

Extended interviews need to take on a dramatic form and structure of their own. Without a sense of drama an interview can degenerate into a tedious ramble up hill and down dale. This is why really good interviewers are valued so highly, and rewarded accordingly.

Don't let the interview just happen

In view of what is written above about spontaneity this might look like a contradiction. This is not so. Guests are perfectly aware that their interview is an artificial construct and normally are willing to fall in with the suggestions of the interviewer. They do after all want to look and sound their best on the box, so it is quite acceptable for the director or interviewer to offer some simple helpful advice. A worthwhile request, which most interviewees will remember and heed without losing the flow, is to try to begin each answer with a statement. For example, if the question is:

'When did you first go to sea?'

the natural answer may begin:

'1940.'

but this is going to be very clumsy to edit, whereas:

'I first went to sea round 1940'

will give the editor a clean entry point and the option of cutting out the interviewer's question without difficulty.

Consider what the guest looks like

It is sometimes important to ask if the guest would mind removing or putting on a jacket or other item of clothing. A dress or shirt might have a hideous check pattern which will strobe on camera, or might contain blue when you are considering chromakey effects. A dark African complexion coupled with a gleaming white shirt can be bad news for a video camera. Bright red dresses can upset electronics and do horrid things to wearers with pale skins. Dress sense is very personal. A director needs diplomatic skills. If spectacles make awkward reflections plead with the guest to remove them. Shiny bald heads and noses can be a problem. Somebody on the unit ought to carry some cosmetic powder, it will be appreciated.

A word of warning

Never, never make promises to a contributor which you may not be able to keep. Never promise that a recorded contribution will definitely be included in the finished programme. A filmed interview can turn into a bore and have to be cut to a few words or ditched altogether in the edit suite. Studio shows often have to drop items for timing purposes. In topical programmes a turn of events can make a story redundant.

Do not promise any guest editorial control. It is best not to let contributors anywhere near a production until it has reached a final stage. Outsiders will not understand a rough cut and want to know why passages seem to have no sound or the interviews are full of jump cuts without cutaways and so on. Better to promise the gift of a cassette after transmission. And make sure the promise is kept and the cassette despatched.

Trick of the trade
There are times when it may be politically necessary to allow a contributor, co-producer or senior executive to see your work at a late stage. It can turn aside wrath and flatter the ego to give them the impression that they have made a positive contribution. Cut the programme to a final duration and in the final form you want, then pick the most boring interview available and reinsert it in an inappropriate place. Let your guest watch the programme without comment and then confess that the picture editor and yourself have done everything possible but that the programme is still running five minutes too long. With luck the visitor will home in on the redundant item which will be revealed to last exactly five minutes. The director and picture editor can express wonder at the acuity of their critic, mutual congratulations exchanged, and further meddling by-passed. The danger is that the invitee may be an idiot, miss the duff take and wants to alter something different. That is the cue for fast talking and quick thinking.

What do you want from the guest?

This brings us back to the fundamental question. Why bother with an interview at all? Some things can only be conveyed honestly or effectively straight from the horse's mouth.

1 Emotion

It is not just unconvincing but possibly untrue to comment that A feels suicidal because of the news of B. Only A can express such a thing. Television has its ghoul school in which intrusiveness masquerades as compassion and whose adherents bully their victims into tears over bereavements, funerals, terminal sickness, murders and disasters. All television journalists ought to swear on oath never to use the question 'How do you feel?' particularly when addressing someone being pulled out of a car crash. It is undeniable that honest emotions, often best recollected in tranquillity, provide the dramatic charge which make many interviews compelling to watch.

2 *Anecdote*

'A once told a story when she was...' is no substitute for the viewer seeing and hearing A tell us personally and directly what happened. The personal tale of someone who claims to have seen little green men emerge from a UFO or was involved in an air crash carries more punch than any editorialized commentary. The immediacy of a personal account cannot be duplicated. A well-told anecdote lifts any kind of interview. Many people are natural storytellers, old people in particular are often a fount of reminiscences. Some of them may even be true.

3 *Opinion*

Unless earlier published statements are quoted it is unconvincing and even defamatory to write:

'Minister "A" agrees unreservedly that...'

or

'Reverend "B" is adamantly against the opinion that...'

The function of many good interviews is to illuminate personal motivation as well as public postures. The mark of many bad ones are grovelling questions which lead only to a reiteration of publicly stated positions. Opinions are most effective if the interview questions tease out personal motives or prejudices. Even the least sympathetic interviewee needs more than some hiccup of a sound bite to reveal a genuine opinion.

4 *Entertainment*

All interviews ought to be entertaining in one way or another but nobody ought to try to tell another man's jokes. An interview can be used as a vehicle for the charm and wit of a guest. The showbiz interview offers a chance to reveal the real person (if one exists) behind the professional performer. It can also be a vehicle for a display of spontaneous, and maybe not so spontaneous, humour. Unfortunately popular entertainers and their agents have nothing to learn from politicians about manipulating television. Often the sole reason for appearing is to plug some new book/recording/film appearance or world tour. All a craven interviewer is required to do is to ask an agent or manager which questions should be offered as cues to spark off a well-rehearsed routine.

Putting the questions

There is a difference between conducting a self-contained live studio interview and recording interview contributions to a documentary. In the former case the interviewer is both an interrogator and a performer. In the latter the intention is often to cut out the interviewer and remove any questions from the sound track. Some basic rules though apply to each.

- Do not use questions which require facts and figures as a reply. Do not, for example, ask a headmaster how many pupils there are in the school, when it went co-educational, the exact cost of the swimming pool, how many GCSEs it has achieved and so on. The interviewer should know all this before even starting the camera. The audience is better presented with statistical information, if it is relevant, from scripted commentary or graphics. An interview is neither a quiz nor an easy alternative to paraphrasing and sub-editing factual information. Interviews are about people. Facts are for scriptwriters. Scriptwriting is a job for professionals.

- Do not ask questions which demand a simple yes or no answer. 'Have you been a member of the Labour Party since the Second World War?' will receive a rather unhelpful reply compared to 'What were your political affiliations?' One bad question tends to lead to another resulting in the interviewer looking dafter and dafter.

  'Is it true that you think airline food is generally disgusting?'
  'Yes.'
  'Surely there have to be exceptions you can think of after all that travelling?'
  'No.'
  'But airline companies will contend that passengers like yourself would be reluctant to pay the increased ticket prices that better catering would lead to, so surely if given the choice you would yourself agree that current standards of in-flight catering as part of an economy travel package represent very reasonable value for money?'
  'I don't agree.'

  When the questions get longer than the answers you are in real trouble.

Trick of the trade

There are some figures whose eminence must be flattered by the offer of an interview. Such guests may have it in mind to use the interview for a personal platform. For example, it can be frustrating to set out to conduct interviews about water problems in the Middle East only to have contributors each start with an irrelevant political tirade about Zionism. In the days of film when stock was expensive this gave rise to the 'Dutch Take' or the 'Rose Coloured Filter'. The crew would go through the actions filming but really not turn over the camera until the director/interviewer gave a sign. Alternatively the guest could rage on until honour was satisfied. The director would call 'Cut', meaning 'Start Recording' and the relaxed question could be put, 'I think that went very well sir, I wonder though if while we're checking you have any thoughts on the long-term water problems of the region?' Another technique, if you know in advance that your guest has a habit of stonewalling or being stricken by panic when an interview begins, is to stage what appears to be a preliminary rehearsal and secretly record that.

- Ask questions simply and one at a time. Tacking main and subordinate questions together or posing a question and then immediately qualifying it can lead to swivel-eyed confusion or frozen panic. The replies are going to be a nightmare to edit at best.

'It has been proposed that the dog population ought to be reduced so would you agree, particularly since research by the Canine Defence League shows evidence that the health risk has been greatly exaggerated, that public opinion might ask should not cats and other animals be included in this category? Where do you stand on budgerigars, for example?'

An old-established acronym for beginners in television is KISS. 'Keep it simple, Stupid.'

Break the questions down logically

'What is the health risk?'
'Is the Canine Defence League evidence correct?'
'What is the risk from other domestic animals?' 'Does that include cage birds?'

• Beware of lists in either questions or answers. It is a hostage to fortune to say, 'I would like to make four basic points' because chances are there will turn out to be five, or both parties will lose track and not be able to remember the fourth.

Never ask questions which include or demand to be answered by lists of statistics. This is the professional vice of television economics correspondents:

'Would you remind us how the pound has fluctuated against the Deutschmark between the '73 oil crisis and Britain leaving the ERM?

If lists and statistics are needed the interview is not the right place to introduce them. Instead write a careful commentary and use plenty of explanatory eye-catching graphics.

• Beware of interrupting. Here is a fundamental difference between directing an interview or discussion in the studio and shooting on location. Interruptions and interjections add life and pace to a studio interview. But most multi camera interviews involve little post production and the ebb and flow of debate is easily covered. On single camera shoots the editing problems must always be in mind. The interviewer should not jump in with supplementary questions or interrupt the guest in full flow unless an answer is going off the rails completely. Do not put the main question but then interject supplementary material as if at a dinner party discussion. This just invites the guest to jump in with a reply before the question is finished with both parties talking at the same time:

'Should the death penalty be restored immediately?...that's the real question...so why are you sitting on the fence like the rest of your party and...'
'That is the most preposterous thing to suggest, my party has never...

'I'd not finished, what I was going to ask...'

Two raised voices talking over each other result in impossible sound edits and are particularly ruinous at the beginning and end of answers where clean sound cuts are needed. The participants may be enjoying themselves but the picture editor will be groping for the Prozac. When this starts to happen it is often best to stop and go for a retake.

- Don't grovel. 'It must have made you truly proud to receive the award in person from Her Majesty...' is not a question, it is a cue for a well-rehearsed stream of self-congratulation. Don't tell people what they may or may not feel and connive at putting the answers into their mouths. Questions beginning 'You must have...' are no good. Sports programmes have a particularly choice repertoire of gormless leading questions demanding equally gormless self-congratulatory or self-exculpatory replies.

Setting the interview

The important subject of an interview is the interviewee. It follows that anything that distracts from the performance of the guest ought to be avoided. Many of the most memorable interviews in television history have been conducted in a pool of light against black or dark grey velour drapes often with low key lighting and extraneous detail dramatically excluded. Such a severe setting demands a lighting cameraman of sensitivity and a directorial decision that this visual style is appropriate to the subject matter. There is a risk of *déjà vu* setting in if this convention is used inappropriately or too frequently. There are good reasons for looking at alternatives.

- Programme identification. This has become increasingly a priority with the expansion of the numbers of channels and very similar looking programmes. Programme producers more and more have to remind the viewers of the name of the programme they are watching and the identity of the channel it is appearing on. One way is to create distinctive set designs featuring recognizable logos and graphics. Studio directors are under pressure to draw attention to the sets.

• Appropriateness of location. A light and insubstantial interview would look out of place in the austere setting suitable for interviewing a professional criminal or the victim of a terminal disease. The lighter the subject matter the more important it is to place the interviewee in a sympathetic setting. This means interviewing a gardener in a garden rather than a kitchen and a lifeboat bo'sun at a quayside or at home surrounded by maritime memorabilia rather than at the betting shop, even though that is where he may spend most of the day. Well-chosen or designed backgrounds can give the viewer a lot of visual information about the interviewee. Naturalistic settings should be identifiable but not obtrusive, whether found on location or designed for the studio. A colonel may best be shown in an officers' mess but a background painting or an impressive piece of mess silver will convey the message. A lot of cluttered mementos, ornaments and flags will distract the eye and add

A word of warning

There have been reporters and directors who failed to understand this. Our lifeboat bo'sun in such hands would likely be asked to put on oilskins and a sou'wester, sit in a dinghy and be interviewed from the top of the harbour wall. Crassness is easiest achieved on location interviews but is not confined to them. Designers and directors of breakfast and daytime programmes may not be averse to filling their sets with chintz curtains and sofas, littering the place with flower arrangements and even providing background effects of birdsong or passing milk vans. Recently directors with short attention spans have discovered Digital Video Effects and are being tempted to fill in the background to interviews with ever-changing graphics or archive footage. An interviewed historian can scarcely utter the word 'Hitler' without an entire Nuremberg rally erupting behind his ear. Unable to concentrate either on the moving lips of the guest or the mouthings of the Fuhrer the poor viewer is cast into electronic chaos. Better to restrict such follies to pop programmes where anything goes and nothing much matters.

nothing to the visual information in the picture. Do not be shy of asking to rearrange the furniture. The object of the interview remains to see and hear the guest to best advantage without distraction.

● Look-mum-I-got-the-job. A location interview may demand a precise geographical setting. The curse of the reporting classes is the compulsion to conduct interviews in front of something which reassures the viewers that they really are (cross-my-heart) where they are supposed to be. Woe to the parliamentary reporter who does not resort to the familiar spots on St Stephen's Green or Millbank with Big Ben against the skyline even though the subject is stag hunting. There are precise spots around the world such as Tiananmen Square in Beijing or the Mount of Olives in Jerusalem where the constant passing of tripods may be responsible for severe environmental damage. This obsession tends to result in reporters or interviewees shot from bizarre angles for the sole reason of getting in some logo, street name or public notice.

Sod's Law also dictates that many of these cliché camera positions are hideously noisy or are right in the path of the public. This can result in bizarrely angled low shots to relate a standing figure and a towering building. A more pleasing composition is usually possibly if the camera is taken back and the figure shot on a narrower lens. The further back the less extreme will be the vertical angle between the lens and the face. Before a director insists on such precise identification of the location it is worth remembering that the most useful shots for an interview are the mid close-up (MCU) and the close-up (CU) and that neither reveal more than a hint of background. An establishing very long shot may be all that is needed or a wide-angle cutaway during the introduction. A quiet easily lit location somewhere with appropriate stonework or greenery in the background can then be found. No drama director would consider compromising picture or sound quality by slavishly trying to represent real geography. Neither should the director of factual programmes.

3

Interviews and cameras

On location

In an ideal world an interview would be conducted with two cameras, one dedicated to the guest and one to the interviewer. The great advantage of conducting interviews in a studio or in an outside broadcast is the access to two or more cameras and the ability to switch instantly between them. With location shoots generally one camera has to suffice. Speed of operation as well as cost considerations dictate this. In all events documentary style programmes depend on a long period of post production and the final shape of the programme will emerge in the cutting room or editing suite. The advantages of a carefully structured multi camera studio interview would be lost if the recording subsequently had to be heavily edited. But a location interview is always shot with editing in mind.

Editing means more than chopping out the bits the director does not like. Editing is a creative process and the picture editor needs to be provided with the means to break down and reassemble questions and answers in various different ways. The picture editor is only going to have this choice if interviews are shot in a way that provides him or her with the wherewithal to make choices. The type of journalist/producer who thinks that the words are all important and the pictures are somebody else's job is arrogant and ignorant.

Over the past decade the common duration for location interviews in magazine programmes has shrunk. Up to the mid-1980s on British television a four or five minute interview was unexceptional. With the arrival of Breakfast TV the maximum shrunk to two and a half minutes. In the 1990s the under twenty second sound bite has become dominant. Fashions change. Still the extended interview retains a place in many programmes. The ability to shoot and edit an interview properly is an essential skill for all television directors.

A word of warning

As cameras have become cheaper and smaller and crew sizes shrunk there is an increasing temptation to shoot locations interviews on two independent (ISO) cameras. This may imply doubling the time to light the set and doubling the time in editing. In theory this should make editing foolproof, but it is not so. Directing two separate cameras is no easier than directing one, often the reverse is true. The director of a multi camera studio has a bank of monitors with which to match his shot sizes and angles and has constant communication with the technical crew. The camera operators may have the facility to switch their viewfinders to see what shots others are offering. The director of two single cameras is blind and mute from the moment the interview begins and the two camera operators cannot communicate with each other. So a very explicit briefing by the director is needed if the two operators are not going to improvise and offer up shots which will never cut together.

Sod's Law dictates that at the most dramatic moment both cameras will simultaneously zoom and refocus, or will each be offering wide two-shots, or be changing tapes. Two cameras may have to compromise their eyelines if they are not going to get in each other's pictures. Double cameras are double trouble. A new director should learn how to direct with a single camera first.

Camera position

Since an interview is usually a matter of two people facing each other the obvious temptation is to place the camera half way between the two of them and pan backwards and forwards according to who is speaking at the time. This doesn't work for three good reasons.

1   Sod's Law states that as soon as the camera has panned to one participant he or she will shut up and the other will start speaking. The camera will be obliged to whip pan back to the speaker where there is a strong chance that the same thing will happen again. The poor operator has only one viewfinder and one set of eyes

and has to rely entirely on hearing as a cue for a camera move from side to side. Inevitably every move will be too late for a good edit. Even worse the best editing points for dialogue are likely to occur in the middle of pans or zooms. Cutting in the middle of pans or zooms always looks horrible.

2   The most revealing facial expressions are in the eyes. A central camera position deprives the viewer of a full view of the faces of either participant and offers at best two half profiles.

3   The pans themselves will look ugly. The space between the two profiles will be either meaningless and empty or else cluttered and distracting. Fast whip pans can be used to get over this but are disorientating. Drama directors can use the two profile set-up but they have the advantage of a prepared script and a rehearsal for every move. The gap between the noses of the two participants can be narrowed by the director. Actors can be positioned far closer face to face than would be comfortable in a real interview, but then they have a script and the time to set and light each camera set-up. A location interview on the other hand often has an element of improvisation and may have to be conducted with a hand-held camera.

The classic single camera set-up

The number of different camera positions and shot sizes which a director might shoot will depend on the anticipated final duration of the story as well as the limitations of the location. The following sequence of camera set-ups will give the optimum number of choices to a picture editor.

First set-up

The priority is to achieve the best camera position to observe the face of the guest. Logically the guest should be able to face the camera lens squarely. This would then give the camera precisely the eyeline of the interviewer. Unfortunately this does not work as the impression is given that the guest is addressing the camera, and so the viewer, direct. The interview becomes a lecture or a soliloquy. During a television interview the viewer should be in the situation of an observer or eavesdropper, not a participant. A direct eyeball-to-eyeball contact becomes uncomfortable. In daily life people rarely square up to each other face to face except in emotionally heightened situations. It is psychologically easier to sit or stand at a slight angle. Note how travellers in a crowded train or lift do their best not to look fellow passengers straight in the eye.

The answer is to position the interviewer as close as possible to one side of the camera lens. If the guest looks at all times at the questioner there will be the best eyeline which is comfortable. The place for the director is behind the camera. This will give the nearest approximate viewpoint as the interviewee, will enable contact with the camera operator and is the best position to hear both questions and answers. The director or producer who wanders off or stands at 90° to the action is just inviting the guest to make distracted sideways glances during the interview. (The same consideration applies where a portable TV monitor is taken on location. It should never be left within sight of the interviewee.) From this position the camera operator should be able to offer a complete range of shots from a mid-shot (MS) to a big close-up (BCU). If the interview is to be a lengthy one and the reporter is significant the editor might also appreciate a two-shot over the reporter's shoulder.

The presenter will have to be careful not to bob around with excitement or go in for florid gestures. There are few things more distracting than seeing bits of arm, ears or shoulders weaving in and out of the television screen. Where the crew has a separate recordist the camera operator ought to define the tightest and widest shots. If this is omitted there is the risk that the recordist will get the microphone in shot or else play safe by keeping well apart and so compromising the sound quality.

Getting the best position is just a beginning. For the best results the camera lens should be exactly on the same level as the eyeline of the guest. This means adjusting the tripod accordingly. The significance of high and low angle shots has been discussed. They can be particularly obvious in the close shots of an interview. Even if eyes and lens are at precisely the same height there can be a problem when the interviewer and guest are also not precisely on a level. A tall standing interviewer putting questions to a short interviewee will result in the latter appearing to roll his eyes towards heaven like a spaniel. When there is a great disparity in heights it is best to abandon any idea of standing interviews and seat the participants. The difference in heights of people is often in the legs rather than the trunk and sitting down can minimize the differences. It is also much easier to find an adjustable chair or prop up one party on cushions than to ask one to stand on an orange box or the other in a trench as sometimes has happened in Hollywood.

Assuming that lighting and sound considerations raise no problems the outstanding question is when and how to change the shot sizes. For a short interview a single mid close-up (MCU) might suffice. Shot sizes need not be changed without some reason; one unvarying shot of an interviewee though can soon make a dull item appear even duller and miss out on the dramatic possibilities presented by an interview. The director who tells the camera operator to 'give me variety of shots' is just avoiding a decision. Far from keeping all the options open until post production it is likely to result in a series of irrelevant and random changes of shot sizes. If the camera operator is not briefed the director has no grounds for complaint when things don't turn out as intended.

Assuming that there is a planned shape to the interview and an agreed set of main questions the camera operator should be able to anticipate at which point to tighten or loosen the shot. As the director should be standing alongside there might be an agreement that the shot changes will take place on a whisper or signal like a light tap on the shoulder. *Shot changes should always take place whilst the interviewer is asking the questions.* The exception is when a lengthy and emotionally charged answer happens and a dramatic slow zoom in vision is obviously appropriate. This ought not to be a surprise to the camera operator. The director and/or journalist should forewarn the camera crew of its likelihood.

Second set-up
Assuming that all has gone well so far the guest might be thanked and released. If the interview is to be part of a feature programme in which the interviewer's questions are to be discarded the interview might end here, otherwise, and as an insurance in most cases, extra camera set-ups will be needed. If possible, prevail upon the guest to stay for a short time.

The camera should move to the opposite side of the set and frame up a shot of the interviewer over the shoulder of the guest. The shots from this second set-up should match those of the first. This means reproducing the same eyeline, in reverse, of the main interview. If the guest was apparently looking slightly left to right in the master shots the interviewee must appear to be looking right to left when recording the questions. The two sets of shots should now intercut seamlessly. You are now in a position to record the questions.

At this point it should be obvious that the interviewer and the director should be able to remember what the original questions were. This is come-uppance time for the journalist who has neither prepared the questions nor stuck to the point, and doom for the director who has insisted on shooting rolls of tape in a vague hope of something good turning up. It is only too frequent to see an entire crew going into an embarrassed huddle trying to remember who said what. Sometimes the only answer is to spool the tape back to the beginning, which is a waste of everyone's time and heavy on the batteries as well. With film this is impossible. Once there is agreement as to what the questions were the inter-viewer must repeat them to camera. A two-shot from behind the guest is very useful particularly if the guest repeats the bodily movements as though beginning to reply at the end of each question. All cuts look better if motivated by even a small movement.

There is no point in cutting the camera between each question unless the interviewer is inept. Cutting can be left until post production. The interviewer can refer to notes between questions or even have them called out from behind the camera. A clean pause at both the beginning and end of each question and a slight facial or bodily movement will be appreciated by the picture editor and make the cuts easier on the eye. When the words are out of the way the guest should be asked to talk naturally whilst the camera concentrates on the reporter. The reporter has nothing to do but react naturally and listen silently and attentively. In this two-shot the guest ought to reproduce much the same head movements and gestures as before and the interviewer has to offer a natural looking range of reactions as though listening. If both of them can achieve this the picture editor will have an ideal set of reverse angles so as to cut between questions and answers or shorten and reassemble the replies.

To be able to ring the changes the interviewer ought to be asked to repeat the questions and offer reaction shots once again, this time for the camera to offer mid-shots and mid close-ups. If the guest is not a masochist he or she will probably beg to leave before this point. In many cases the guest will have left immediately after the end of the final answer and so two-shots are out of the question and close-up questions and reaction cutaways of the interviewer may be the only ones possible. It is hard for even a seasoned presenter to simulate an eyeline and convincingly react to thin air. It is very helpful for the director or a crew member to take the place of the missing guest. If the interviewer is with a one-man crew one solution is for the camera operator to hold out his free hand to the correct side of the camera and for the journalist to take an eyeline from that.

Trick of the trade

There are occasions where an interview has to be conducted on the terms of the interviewee, the questions will be all unintelligibly off-camera and the answers obviously in need of heavy editing. These are also the most likely occasions for the guest to dismiss the crew after the final reply without there being any possibility of shooting cutaways on the location. Under the circumstances it is best to log the questions by later replaying the videotape and then reconstructing them. A little improvement to the wording might be appropriate in view of the recorded replies. All that is needed now is a background which will intercut convincingly with that seen behind the interviewee. These cutaway questions and reactions can be recorded somewhere completely different or even some considerable time later. One of the most difficult things to remember after a time lapse is whether the interviewee was originally looking left or right. It may be impossible to refer back to the original rushes. The belt and braces solution to the dilemma is to record the questions and reaction shots twice, once looking in each direction. The most likely give-away to this little deception is a wildly unmatched background microphone acoustic.

Finally, in mid close-up, the interviewer should mime a series of mute reactions appropriate to the content of the recorded answers. These are the dreaded 'noddies' which have done more than anything to bring location interviews into disrepute. Even professional performers can be reduced to horrid grimaces and nervous tics when they are asked to do something as simple as look amused or make a knowing nod of the chin. Most noddies go straight to the proverbial cutting room floor. They are though the ultimate insurance policy, take almost no time to do and have saved many a desperate picture editor from despair. If you have time always record some of them.

Extra set-ups

The picture editor should by now have more than enough material. However, there are some further possibilities. Questions should be short, to the point, and not need shortening. But there are times when an unprofessional interviewer waffles on in a way that cries out for cutting. In this case a reaction shot of the guest will be needed. This might exist already on the first recording as the guest was listening to the ramblings of the interrogator. But as questions are asked at the time when the camera is most likely to be zooming or refocusing these shots may be spoiled. If the director anticipates trouble in the editing it may be useful to have some cutaway reaction shots of the guest. In which case they should be recorded immediately after the main interview – shoot them in mid-shot and mid close-up. Get the interviewer to ask any sort of question but warn the guest to listen but not answer. Some directors prefer to 'steal' these cutaways during the informal chat before the main recording.

Over-the-shoulder two-shots and mid-shots should be wide enough to reveal the background in most locations. There are times though which cry out for placing figures in a landscape. Interviews in the grounds of famous buildings or a dramatic landscape would be examples. In such cases a very wide two-shot is called for. This means an extra camera set-up and as the participation of the interviewee is essential this is sometimes best done at the very beginning of the shoot. The wide shot can be anything that the director wants with two essential provisos:

1   The figures must be distant enough and framed so

that the viewer is not able to read any lip movements.
2   The figures must actually be talking in turn so that discernible head and body movements will match the shots in the actual interview.

If the guest has agreed to wait until the end for these wide shots the director may be tempted to retake one or two questions with synchronous sound on this wide angle. The

A word of warning

In a studio it is possible for the director to repeatedly readjust and match shots on all cameras during the course of an interview. For example, if the director decides to tighten or widen the shot of a guest it is possible to change the framing likewise of the interviewer on another camera during a subsequent answer. The cuts will be more pleasing as a result. This is far harder to achieve with a single camera as the final assembly order of question and answer may not be decided at the time of the shoot. So it is tempting to leave everything to the camera operator.

The danger of the 'just give me a variety of shots' school of non-direction is that the framing of questions and answers may brutally clash at the edit. A question in big close-up (BCU) cut to a reply in a loose two-shot, for example, will look awful. The effect is particularly nasty where the producer wants to splice together parts of two different replies to construct a single statement. If the two halves are in wildly different framings and a noddy is all that is available to soften the jump cut there is complete visual disorientation. The camera operator and the director have to work as a team on interviews. Remember the basic grammar:

1   the tighter the shot the more dominant the subject
2   the guest is always more important than the interviewer

It is important that when the interview is assembled the shots of the interviewer should never be closer and more dominant than those of the guest. Conversely a shot of an interviewer which is looser than that of the subsequent answer is normally acceptable.

> ### Trick of the trade
>
> Many interviews will require lighting. If time is pressing it can be tiresome to have to move the tripod and reset all the lights for the reverse-angle questions and reaction shots. To avoid this simply put the interviewer in the same chair as the guest and slightly change the background, for example pulling curtains, moving a desk or altering the decor. Moving either the performer or the camera a mere metre left or right can often do the trick. The audience has no idea of the real geography of the location and so long as nothing like an identical painting in both backgrounds gives the game away they will accept the deception. A similar trick is usual on outside locations where the interviewee has been placed in a position with an attractive background but where the interviewer necessarily has his back to brightly lit or distracting scenery. It is though vital to recall that if the interviewee was looking left to right then the interviewer must give a matching eyeline looking right to left.

problem is sound quality. Radio mics often have very different characteristics to other microphones and the sound perspective of the wide shot may sound unnatural when cut with the close-ups. The wide shots and the close-ups do not have to be taken in the same spot. A quiet corner of a garden might serve best for an interview whilst the most pleasing lighting and composition for the wide shot might entail moving the participants round to the front of the house. So long as someone keeps a close eye on continuity the viewer will be none the wiser. General greenery or appropriate stone or brick is safe. The more specific the visual references the harder it is to cheat. Beware of the pot plants which come and go between shots.

Other locations

The classic interview technique allows for the guest and interviewer to be either sitting or standing. This is the normal way of holding a conversation and minimizes any distraction on the television picture, though often directors are attracted by the idea of conducting interviews on the move. If the subject is, for example, gardening or architecture or life on the streets it can be much more revealing for the two participants to be found walking side by side through the location and chatting to each other. If the location and subject matter have no immediately obvious connection the technique can be rapidly very irritating. Viewers' reaction is 'Stand still will you!'

An interview does not become automatically more appealing because the director has become bored and decided to pep things up by having the camera and the participants roaming about. Unlike the classic static interview the key shot in a walking interview is not the guest but the frontal two-shot. This is taken either from directly in front of the camera or from slightly to one side favouring the guest. A lot will depend on how big is the role of the interviewer and how much background the director wants to reveal. Unless the production is prestigious enough to afford a professional dolly on rails with a grip to operate it the camera operator has to hand hold the camera. This opens up a whole new set of problems.

1   The operator is going to be walking backwards. Assuming that the location is not devoid of trees, kerbstones, molehills, passers-by or buses, health and safety considerations suggest that someone should be behind him or her keeping an eye out for hazards and steering by a hand on the shoulder or belt strap. With a three-man film crew this is the job of the camera assistant. In the case of the two-man video crew the recordist may have to serve. The trouble is that moving interviews are very likely to present sound problems and it takes Houdini-like abilities to monitor sound, hold a directional microphone and walk crabwise looking backwards. So the director gets the job. With the cost-cutting journalist plus one-camera set-up it may be best to abandon the idea rather than risk appalling sound quality and a broken ankle. An alternative is to place the camera on the tripod and have the performers walk forward into a two-shot. This will preserve the camera operator for another day but might present

focus difficulties. The recordist will need radio microphones.

2   Wherever possible there should be a rehearsal or a careful walk through with the camera. Performers walking forward will tend to go much faster than a camera crew walking backwards and any severe mis-match of pace will at the least wreck the focus or at worse have them over-running the camera.

3   Lighting can be critical in walking interviews. Above all the camera should try to avoid shooting into a brightly lit background or the open sky. If the background has changeable lighting the operator will very likely have the video camera set to an automatic iris. Even the best video camera is not quick or smart enough to match the eye against severely changing light conditions. Exposures are likely to see-saw up and down between over- and underexposed backgrounds. Nobody should be deceived by the brilliantly lit backgrounds in cinema films or television drama. These generally have the benefit of huge lighting rigs to balance their foregrounds and are shot on film which is much better at handling lighting contrast than the most advanced video. If the contrasts are significant it may be possible to light the performers' faces with a battery lamp or reflector. This in turn will oblige the camera to shoot close up excluding much of the background and very likely defeating the object of the exercise.

4   Walking shots, like pans or zooms, benefit from having a definite beginning and end. This is another reason why a camera rehearsal is needed. In the case of a short interview it is visually pleasing to have the performers come to a halt at an arranged mark to complete the item on a static two-shot. A pause to comment on some object or scene which demands a cutaway gives a neat ending. An alternative, depending on what scene comes next, is to bring the camera to a halt and allow the participants to pass by through the frame. This is the solution if the intention is to continue the interview with further walking shots or if the next scene

discovers the same performers in a static situation or in a different location.

5   For a short while the frontal two-shot will suffice but if an extended interview is anticipated there will be a need for a variety of shots. It is possible to shorten the walking interview with cutaways, particularly if the guest halts from time to time to point out something. But static cutaways dropped into a moving interview always look crass. The best cutaways are those representing the point of view of the guest and tracking at the same speed as the walk. A moving shot will then cut seamlessly to a matched moving shot. Estimating the speed of two walks is easier said than done. If the interviewee is judged capable of repeating a performance the director should take reverse-angle questions and cutaways just as in a classic static interview but on the move. The moving backgrounds will have to match those in the wide two-shot. The camera operator will walk sideways to the action. The performers will have to match the speed of the original walk and repeat any stops or turns.

Trick of the trade
It would make life much easier if instead of trying to walk backwards as fast as the performers walking forward, the camera operator could make them keep to his or her own speed. When the distance between the camera lens and the presenter or interviewer is critical for focus this is essential. To ensure that distance is constant and walking speed synchronous an assistant walks alongside the camera holding an ordinary broom with the bristle end pressed firmly into the midriff of the performer. The performer keeps pressing against the broom and so can neither over-run the camera nor drop back out of focus.

Car interviews

A variation on the walking theme is the interview in a moving vehicle. In some ways car shots present fewer problems than walking ones. The camera has to be in a static position on a wide lens angle. There is very little scope for any zooming and panning and rarely any need. The interviewee is normally in the driving seat and so physically fixed in place. Once the balance of the voice with engine noise has been set the sound problems are few. With only minimal extra lighting a successful car interview can be recorded in cities at night. There are problems, however:

1   A driver, if he knows what's good for him, keeps his eyes on the road ahead with occasional sideways glances at the passenger. A camera in same eyeline as the passenger seat will be restricted to profiles and half profiles.
2   Most vehicles are too small to allow the interviewer as well as a camera in front alongside the driver.
3   The moving background through the driver's window will present the same contrast problems as in walking interviews with even less predictability or chances for rehearsal.

The choice of solution to these problems is, as always, dictated by the time and budget available. The most acceptable two-shot would be through the front windscreen, though reflections are going to present a major problem. There are various mountings available for hire which allow a camera to be mounted on the bonnet of a car looking backwards. The simplest of these is a rubber sucker type limpet mount. With even such simple gear the production ought to hire the services of a grip to install and make safe the mount. A camera flying loose towards a windscreen or into passing traffic does not bear thinking about. The surest way to achieve head-on shots is to mount the whole car onto a low-loading trailer which is the towed through the location. All the driver has to do is simulate appropriate steering wheel turns and gear changes. There is a choice of positions for the camera on the trailer itself or the rear of the towing vehicle.

A two-shot, or matching single shots, can be achieved by mounting a camera to look through the side windows from outside. There is an enormous range of car mounts available. Some use the latest generation of miniature cameras and exciting new possibilities have opened up, some pioneered by sports programmes, some a spin-off of medical technology. Other mounts involve complex harnesses to take both camera and camera operator. It is not safe to use any of these on a public highway and rental firms will advise the hire of a grip to accompany the equipment. This is all very desirable but most interviews fit into the bargain basement end of the television spectrum. The hand-held camera is all that is available. The following configuration is safest.

The camera operator crouches in the well of the front passenger seat looking upwards at the driver. Most of the side window and part of the windscreen may be in vision. The interviewer sits in the rear offside passenger seat. In order to respond to questions the driver will incline to keep looking over the shoulder rather than just glancing sideways and with luck will present the camera with occasional full face close-ups. There is often no room for both a recordist and director to share the remaining back seat. The recordist ought to take precedence.

Car interviews, even short ones, frequently require editing. Cars offer a multitude of cutaways which take little time and should always be taken after the interview has finished. Hands on gear shifts, indicator switches and lights, close-ups of eyes in mirrors, feet on pedals, etc. are obvious choices. Apart from any showing a moving background through the driver's window most of these shots can be simulated in a stationary vehicle after the end of the interview. Nobody will ever know.

Trick of the trade

Why waste petrol? Just as most driving sequence cutaways are better mocked up in a static car so sometimes is the main action. If the background through the window is simple sky (assuming the contrast problems can be overcome) there is no way an audience can tell whether a car is moving or not. Engine sound effects and the performer looking fixedly at a windscreen will tell them that it is. The slight movement achieved by someone rocking the car will do the rest. At night the impression of movement can be achieved by panning a hand-held light past the windows. You will not get away with it for long but you can save a lot of time and money. To simulate a dismal night wonders can be worked using a lawn sprinkler on the windscreen wipers...but now our interview is turning into a drama, as sometimes perhaps it ought.

> **Words of warning**
>
> Crossing the line is a problem in static and walking interview cutaways. It is critical in car shots. The driver can only be shot from one side and all other shots should replicate this apparent direction of movement. Cutting to a point of view shot through the passenger side window would give the effect of the car crashing into instant reverse. If the interior shots are to match with exterior ones the tripod has to be placed so the vehicle passes to the correct side of the camera. So if the close-up of the driver with moving background appears to be moving left to right, so should the vehicle seen from the pavement. Even in feature films the director has problems with cross shooting dialogue in a moving vehicle as although the two eyelines may be matched the backgrounds will appear to be reversing their direction of movement with each cut. Life is made simpler by keeping the interviewer out of vision.

Additional cutaways are provided by finally putting the camera on a tripod outside and getting the vehicle to drive past. It is unlikely that the viewer will be able to make out who is driving or even how many people are inside. What goes for cars goes for aircraft although the safety considerations and space restrictions are even more critical.

Two for the price of one

The interview situations described so far have involved two participants only (the one plus one interview). It is possible to try including two interviewees at a time, and sometimes if the director is feeling adventurous, three or more. There are times when this can produce good results, occasionally moving but generally hilarious. The first requirement is that the interviewees should be equally animated and react to each other throughout. The best results will be obtained by interviewing, for example, a group of sparky girls in a night-club, an eternally bickering married couple or any other naturally occurring double act. The one plus two interview shot on a single camera must be approached with caution. It offers many hostages to fortune.

1   The only safe shot for the cameraman is the two-shot of the interviewees. A two-shot is only sustainable whilst there is a lively response between the characters on camera. It can quickly pall.

2   If one character starts a soliloquy the temptation is for the camera to zoom into a close-up shot. Sod's Law is then bound to strike and the other person will start talking. The choice is then between a sudden zoom back to the two-shot, which will look very odd, or a whip pan to the other interviewee who will unerringly shut up just as the camera has framed up.

3   Editing two-shots to cut out unwanted material leads to very unpleasant jump cuts. The only likely cutaway, as in a normal interview, would be mid close-up or mid-shot of the interviewer. This will work but the contrast between the close-up and the wide two-shot may be clumsy. Two-shot interviews are best cut short.

4   Last but not least, psychology rears its head. When two people in vision talk alternately the attention of the viewer switches back and forth accordingly; but only for a short time. It is human nature to pay attention to the silent party as well as the vocal one. If the non-speaking one does anything distracting, has a nervous tic or even stands there like a zombie the viewers' attention rapidly drifts away from the speaking member of the duo. Unwittingly the non-speaker will be pulling the old actors' trick of upstaging the other.

All of which is to say that the safest and best way to interview more than one person at a time is to shoot them with multi camera facilities either in a television studio or on an outside broadcast.

Note

There are many directors who have become appalled by inept cutaways and noddies that they have abandoned them altogether. There is the argument that since everyone ought to be aware that location interviews are shortened and reassembled it is only honest to reveal the cuts to the viewers.

It is very much a matter of taste. There is no perfect solution. Removing noddies, reverse-angle questions and similar cutaways means that any editing will result in jump cuts. Even the most wooden interviewee changes head position and facial expression constantly whilst talking. The director has a choice.

1   Accept the jump cuts as they are. This can work with an impassive guest and depends on the interview being conducted in one single framing. Jump cuts between different shot sizes are usually more disturbing than the clumsiest noddy. The exception is that it is sometimes possible to have a jump cut from a wider shot to a much tighter one down the same axis. It all depends on the angle of the heads being similar and the mouth being either open or closed in each.

2   Take the edge off the jump cut by using a quick dissolve between the frames. This is probably the least visually disturbing solution and again its effectiveness will depend on the similarity of the incoming and outgoing shots. Too fast a dissolve looks like a jump cut gone wrong; too long and the cut can induce something like a sense of passing nausea in the viewer.

3   Draw attention to the edit by inserting several blank white frames or by a fade down to a black screen and up again. There was a period in the 1980s when this was very much in vogue. This works very well with extended interviews which have obviously been shot over a long time or even on different occasions. Slow fades traditionally have implied a passage of time in the cinema. As a result the pace

Trick of the trade
It can be quicker in the editing if the answers are shot on one cassette and the questions and cutaways on another. When time is the main consideration the interview can be constructed as best as possible from assembling the answers of the guest and dropping in any necessary cutaways afterwards. A problem can arise if the original questions are different and longer than the ones repeated for the reverse angle shots.

of the interview will be slowed down and if the subject matter demands fast cutting the fades become dreary.

4   Cover the cuts with an electronic transition, anything from a simple wipe to a starburst or to any one of the breathtaking digital effects now available. This has the advantage of covering up at a stroke all the editing problems and continuity mistakes made on location. Possibly appropriate in the context of frothy entertainment shows or children's programmes.

Word of warning

Directors mesmerized by words sometimes take refuge in trying to edit interviews from typed transcripts. Transcripts have a place in long documentary series constructed from many long interviews. But they only are a guide to subject matter, not a blueprint for cuts. A transcript tells you nothing about expression, shot size, tone of voice or pace of delivery. An interview edited from a transcript alone will just pile up shots that cannot be cut together. This is particularly so if the director tries to treat television as radio and cut about from sentence to sentence in order to reconstruct the replies. The mis-use of noddies has frequently come about because of attempts to twist the pictures to fit words selected from a printed page.

4

Into the studio

Multi camera interviews

An interview in a studio presents enormous advantages over one shot on location. So long as there is space and adequate cameras and lighting a studio interview may involve two, three or almost any number of guests. At a certain point though the show ceases to be an interview and turns into a chaired discussion. The simplest definition of the difference is that a discussion is when the number of participants exceeds the number of cameras available.

A really skilled director with a lively professional camera crew can make a creditable job of directing a one plus three interview on just a couple of cameras. A complete dullard ought to be safe with four cameras for four performers. It just ought to be obvious that with one camera for one performer things cannot go wrong. Like most obvious things about television, it is not true.

A location interview is always shot with post production editing in mind. It should be shot in such ways as to present the picture editors with the best possible variety of shots. In the studio the opposite is true. A large number of interviews are conducted live, or recorded as if live. There may be a possibility of video tape editing to remove embarrassing or libellous answers or to insert retakes but this is not the object. The director should aim to work to an allotted time and complete an interview item entire without a thought of editing.

A director of a location interview can try to sidestep making any creative decisions beyond choosing the questions and hope the story will be saved by camerawork, picture editing, and dollops of luck. In the studio interview the director is the totally in charge and there is no passing the buck.

Unlike most single camera productions the studio director rarely has much input into the editorial content of an interview. The decision that A is going to spend six minutes interviewing B about subject C is about as far as it goes. This does not mean that he or she can then put both feet up on the gallery desk until transmission time and wait to see what fate will bring. This may happen on tired series which repeat an identical format week after week: and it shows. The director's hands are pretty much tied if the journalist or producer responsible for the item does not take the director into confidence about the intended style of interview. What editorial matter goes into the interview is a job for producers; how it comes over is the director's department.

A good interview stands out. Like all other kinds of studio direction a good interview depends on meticulous pre-production planning. By the time the guest is ushered onto the set it is too late to do anything much but busk through the performance.

Planning the interview

The producer

The producer may be ignorant of the requirements of a director. Many producers today have only journalistic backgrounds. Few have worked as directors. The title of Producer has been steadily broadened and diminished throughout television in recent times and often now designates not the most senior but the least experienced member of the team. The director may have to pester the producer for information. There are some basic questions to be asked.

1   *What type of interview is it?* What is the subject and has the producer got any kind of agenda which can influence the style of direction? The name of a guest says nothing. A proposed interview with one well-known MP might just as easily bear upon his voting record in Parliament, his attitude to the European Union, his commercial involvement with arms manufacturers, his great personal wealth, his well-publicized support for a football team, his day job as a disc jockey or his celebrated sex life. Presumably the producer intends to focus on just one or two of these.

2   *What mood is to be created?* If the focus is on the football and the extramarital junketing should the interview take the form of an interrogation on the

state of public morality or a jolly chat about the off-duty activities of public figures?

3   *Who is asking the questions?* If an interviewer is well known it may be as well to get past the producer and ask him or her about the editorial content. If this is going to be an in-depth interview presumably there is some intended structure.

There are questions which seem to have nothing to do with the producer but can easily make a vast difference to the direction. A decent producer or researcher will always be on the lookout for these things and inform the director. Just don't bet on it happening.

1   *Does the guest have any disabilities? (this is no place for political correctness)* Are there squints, scars, glass eyes or even the effects of old age which suggest a preference for one profile or the other? Should the director avoid close-ups? Ageing celebrities are not squeamish and often know the business. They may demand to be shown from a certain side and even with a particular lighting or use of soft focus filters.

2   *Does the guest normally use wild gesticulations in conversation?* The director does not want to be caught in close-ups with heads and hands bobbing in and out of shot or of focus.

3   *Does the guest smoke?* If smoking is allowed on set, where is the ashtray? If it is forbidden who is going to do the explaining?

4   *Does the guest intend to bring any objects or printed material to the interview?* Will it be for demonstration purposes or simply for display? If a politician is intending to bring a government paper to the studio it makes all the difference whether he intends to wave it about during a debate (wide shots), is to make it a point of repeated references (cutaways) or is insisting on reading extracts from it (over the shoulder close-ups).

5   *Is the guest likely to stand up or give any sort of a performance during the interview?* This will affect both sound and lighting. No favours will be done if a comedian leaps to his feet for an animated

performance of a gag and vanishes into obscurity and silence because the only lit area is around a table and the only microphones are pointing at the chairs.

The studio set

The director's control over the design may be considerable or it may be nearly non-existent. Long running series may have sets which are inflexible and only updated at long intervals. Single programmes will have specially designed sets and the director should have a big input into design decisions at the planning stage of production. Most sets have some built-in flexibility so that background flats, drapes, and dressing properties can be rearranged on the day. The key feature is the studio lighting. Excellent interviews can be conducted with no set at all apart from chairs, a table and well-done studio lighting. Studio lighting is an art and takes time. The producer or director who starts making last minute major alterations to the set or seating plan is going to make no friend of the lighting supervisor.

The world of the digitally created virtual set has arrived and will soon dominate many types of magazine programme where interviews are prominent components. Whether this electronic marvel has the flexibility required for imaginative studio direction remains to be seen. Assuming that the director's voice is going to be heard the following considerations are important.

1   *Is the set muted in colour and tone?* The plainest designs can be enhanced by creative lighting but the most lurid or fussy resist any reinterpretation. The dress sense and colour preferences of guests cannot be taken for granted. The more assertive the set the more likely a hideous colour clash with the guests' outfits.

2   *Is there an obligation to show programme logos or programme names?* If these are an integral part of the set the seating has to be arranged so these graphics appear in the middle of wide shots or carefully framed behind the two-shots. A logo wobbling half in and half out of any shot is just distracting.

3   *Are there obvious vertical or horizontal lines in the design?* Set designers are often trained architects

and look at their constructions on the whole like stage sets (the author's apologies to those who know better). Strong verticals are difficult to avoid with a set constructed of stage flats. Horizontals give a unity to studio sets when shown in wide shots. But there is nothing more distracting than a close-up where a performer has a vertical line appearing out of the top of the head or a horizontal one going in one ear and out the other.

4   *Does the design involve back projection, photo blow-ups or complex set dressing?* These may look spectacular from the studio floor or in a wide shot. They may be essential to the programme content. But if they are dimly perceived and out of focus they can ruin the composition of singles and two-shots. The old truth must be repeated. Interviews are about people. People means close pictures of faces. Anything which unnecessarily distracts from the human face is irrelevant.

Studio furniture

The influence of the director on the overall design of the set may be small. Decisions about arranging the set are another matter. Even the smallest station should possess a variety of furniture for interviews.

1   Almost all studio interviews take place seated. The choice of chairs is then of prime importance. They must look good on camera. It is the job of the designer to provide these. They must be comfortable. Exquisitely designed Bauhaus inspired steel chairs may create an aesthetic whole with the total design concept of the set, at least in the opinion of a designer, but they are damn-all use to the director if after two minutes the guests start wriggling on their bums with discomfort. Chairs must not though be too comfortable. They must keep the occupants performers' backs upright and prevent them swaying or lounging about.

2   Crossed legs or legs stretched out straight in front result in very unattractive camera shots. So are knees

bunched up under chins particularly when the guests are wearing short skirts. Chairs should be high enough to prevent this happening.

3   Adjustable height chairs are ideal. They are the quickest way to equalize great height disparities between performers. Unfortunately most are manufactured as swivel chairs. Always lock any such chairs in one position, except for discussion presenters who may wish to swing from one eye-line to another during a debate. It is curiously surreal to watch a close-up of a guest whose eyes and head appear steady in the frame whilst the body and shoulders revolve back and forth on a swivelling chair.

4   If cosy sofas and armchairs are stipulated make sure that the studio cameras can get proper eyelines. Camera mountings have a limit to how low they can operate and someone slumped on a sofa is likely to sit below them. One solution is to have the seating area raised on rostra, otherwise hard cushions can be used prop up the guests.

5   When using rostra be careful that there are enough of them. Too great an area of rostra will impede the cameras in a small studio. Too small an area and the risk is that a long limbed guest will stick their legs out over the front of the stage or propel themselves backwards and over the edge. Rostra in the darkened television studio are a well-recognized safety hazard.

Positioning the participants

The studio interview set-up is the perfect place to demonstrate the need for television grammar. The simple matter of rearranging the position of seats on a set can radically affect the viewers' perception of an interview. The seating should naturally be in harmony with the set design. It is hard to conduct a tough face-to-face interrogation about police corruption if the interviewee is sitting in a comfy armchair or the interviewer has a flight of plaster ducks going up the wall in his background. But just how the two face each other makes the greatest difference. Consider four basic possibilities.

1 *The confrontation*

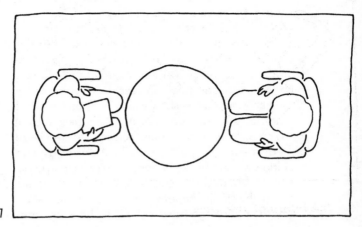

Figure 4.1

The situation is one of interrogation. The protagonists face each other eyeball to eyeball over a table (Figure 4.1). The seating forces the interviewee to face the interviewer directly at all times and any attempt to look away will appear furtive or desperate in the eyes of the viewers. This is the interview situation which demands the minimum of set in vision and is best conducted in a pool of light with low key lighting against a totally black background, only a neutral coloured circular carpet or low table ought to separate the two. Everything is weighted against the guest. The impression of nose-to-nose confrontation can be heightened by pulling the two main cameras as far back as possible and shooting on the end of the zoom. This is most effective in two-shots.

2 *The formal interview*
The situation is still one of interrogation but the odds are not heavily weighted against the guest (Figure 4.2). The chairs are set at an approximate angle of 90° and if there are desks they should be separated and identical in size. Normal high key lighting is appropriate though an uncluttered back-ground is still desirable, apart perhaps for a programme logo. The feeling should be one of respectfully serious debate between equals.

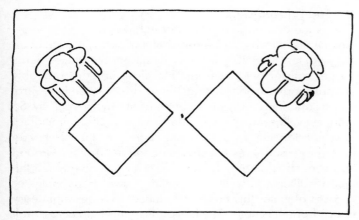

Figure 4.2

3 The informal interview

Figure 4.3

The assumption here is a relationship of greater informality. It is not suitable for earth shaking subject matter. The chairs are placed around an oval table or curved desk so that the participants can turn to address each other informally whilst not ruining the close-up camera eyelines (Figure 4.3). The use of the single table suggests a warmth between the participants. The curved table is suitable if two or more guests are to be introduced.

4 The relaxed chat

This is the appropriate set-up for lightweight programmes. The chairs, which may be armchairs or sofas, are set at an angle of less than 90°, as widely as still enables the cameras to get satisfactory close-ups. Big close-ups are probably inappropriate in this setting; there are frequently several guests and there may be an amount of physical activity. So perfect eyelines may have to be sacrificed. The definition of a satisfactory close-up is simple. So long as the viewer can clearly see both eyes the shot is adequate. Any foreground furniture should be in the form of a low coffee table. If the guest is likely to use this for putting down props, notes or glasses of water this has to be placed upstage within easy reach from the chairs. The less participants lean across shot the better. This is the informal set-up with the greatest risk of guests slowly vanishing into the upholstery with knees dominating the foreground and heads vanishing into rucked-up jacket collars.

Lining up shots

When the director has winkled out of the producer the intentions of the interview and has briefed the designer, lighting and sound supervisors, it is time to consider the cameras. Everything is now up to the director. Whether or not there is a studio floor plan the director should have envisaged what shots are going to be needed and whether these are likely to present any problems for the camera crew. It is much better to be able to tell the cameras which shots will be needed than begin by asking which shots they can offer.

There should be no problem with a simple one-plus-one interview. The only difficult bits are at the beginning and end. At the beginning cameras may need to rehearse a sequence for introducing the participants. At the end there may be a programme formula involving lighting changes and music for signing off. During a live show the director may have to release some of the cameras to the next set-up during the closing part of the interview.

An interview can be shot with only one well-directed camera (if the situation is desperate) but normally there are two, three, four or more cameras. The essential points to keep in mind are:

1   The director has to make clear the physical relationship between the two participants and the studio. An interview exclusively comprising close-ups would be confusing. The viewer needs some reference to the studio and the physical positioning of the performers. This is particularly true when there is more than a single interviewee.

2   The viewer needs to be able to see each of the participants full face in the close-ups.

Before starting rehearsal the director should make some final checks.

Has the furniture been set on the arranged marks? Many a director has been bamboozled about why his shots do not seem to work when the problem was that chairs had been dumped down only more or less in the right place or shifted by the participants. It is the job of the floor manager to keep an eye out for this. But in these economy conscious times not all studios have an FM.

Is it clear who is sitting where and is this clear from any camera script or programme running order? If the interview involves more than one guest and a shot is described as 'Three-shot Tom/Dick/Harry' it means Tom is on the left, Dick is in the middle, and Harry is on the right. The technical crew needs to know who is who. A last minute realignment when an interviewer tetchily wants to be on one familiar side or a guest arrives wearing an eyepatch can upset things. It is easier to say:

'Camera one, close-up of Tom'

than

'Camera one get me a close-up of that MP, the fat one in the pin stripe suit in the middle.'

Setting up the shots for an interview does not need the interviewee to be present on the studio floor. Even if the guest is in the building it will be quicker and easier to get on with lining up the shots in his absence. The participants are probably busy with the producer and interviewer or else with make-up. Get the floor manager and another colleague to sit in for them. This is the final opportunity for adjusting lighting and sound. The director is only now in a position to run through the camera shots.

Always plan to cross shoot

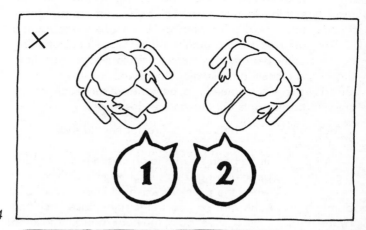

Figure 4.4

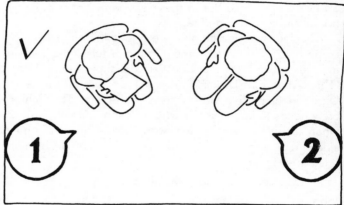

Figure 4.5

This should be glaringly obvious. The only way to get satisfactory eyelines is to place the main cameras opposite each other getting the fullest face shots as are compatible with not getting each other in frame. Inexperienced directors find themselves in a situation where all their cameras get bunched together in the middle of the studio searching for workable shots on their own halves of the stage. This impossible to direct situation results from not paying attention to what is being shown on the camera monitor screens in the gallery, and not doing a proper run-through.

Are the two sit-ins taking things seriously? They must offer the same eyelines as are anticipated during the real recording. If they swivel round or turn their heads to chat to friends in the crew the camera line-up will be worthless.

The cameras may appear to be correctly positioned on the studio floor but this does not always guarantee that the shots match each other. In serious one-plus-one interviews this may be particularly important. The way of checking is to line up two-shots on the cameras. The apparent distance between the two participants should seem the same in both over-the-shoulder shots and a frontal wide shot. Rather than lining up each camera in turn the director should line up the shots on the camera which favours the guest, and ask the remaining cameras to adjust their own framing to that.

Match the height of eyelines. A good camera operator will always adjust the pedestal height to the eyeline of the subject. If the worst happens at the last moment and the guest turns out to be seven foot tall while the interviewer is a mere five footer the director must readjust and try to simulate the actual eyelines. The camera covering the close-up of a tall subject will have to lower slightly, that on the shorter will have to go slightly up to match. Otherwise the taller may appear to be glancing modestly at the ground whilst the shorter will gaze slightly upwards in awe or inspiration.

Shot sizes will have to be matched. The latitude sometimes allowed in single camera reports does not extend to the studio. Politicians in particular are aware of how a star interviewer can be given undue prominence by unequal shot sizes.

Direct the cameras to positions where they can offer a well-framed range of shots, wide two-shots to big close-ups, without having to change position in order to avoid shooting each other or off the edge of the set. This may have to involve some compromise. The ideal eyelines possible with a single camera may not be possible when several are involved. But studio camera mountings can do some things a tripod cannot. They can move to a new position, and with a good operator they can move very fast. They need a warning that they might be asked to do so, and preferably a rehearsal.

If there is a third camera available for a one-plus-one do not waste it on a single wide two-shot to show the set at the beginning and end of the interview. In between times it can crab either way to offer interesting alternative two-shots or additional close-ups of the guest. The greater the number of cameras and interviewees the greater the variety of possible shots and the more the studio will need to be actively directed.

An interview has to be impromptu and 'as directed' but beginnings and endings can and ought to be rehearsed. There is generally a scripted introduction and frequently a standard programme format for the ending. The crew, the interviewer and the floor manager all need to know the shot sequence. It is not unknown to see a presenter talking to the wrong camera or wretchedly staring around for the one with a red light on. This sticks out like a sore thumb to the least perceptive viewer.

Helpful hint

With interviews to be recorded for later insertion into a main programme it is safest to start and end the interview by holding a shot of the guest. It may be necessary at a later stage to rewrite the introduction as a studio hand-over link. In news magazine programmes the interviewer may also double up as anchor in the studio and there is a risk of a reorganized running order leaving him handing over in vision to himself. There is always a risk of comedy when one presenter hands over to another in vision.

Sandra	Thank you, Sir George. And now back to Fred in the studio.
Fred	Thank you, Sandra. And now the latest weather from Tracey.
Tracey	Thank you, Fred. Well the deep depression over...

Line up the main shots and check the composition at all times. There is no point in insisting on a particular shot if the camera has to sacrifice looking room or head room in order not to shoot off the set. The director should know what shots are required but it is always worth listening and watching for suggestions from the cameras. In busy programmes with several contributors or unfamiliar sets there might be a little winner of a shot which had not been anticipated.

If the opening shots include a wide one showing the whole set and all participants, the director should line this shot up first. This will enable the other cameras to position themselves out of shot, unless it is the programme style to deliberately show cameras, sound booms and lighting rigs. This has to be clear from the start. The audience is quite used to programmes which cheerfully reveal the technology. What is ridiculous is the sight of an unexplained microphone swinging through shot or the sight of a camera scurrying about trying to hide out of the way.

Cutting interviews

In prestigious programmes there is often a vision mixer (switcher) in addition to a studio director present in the gallery (control). In low budget programmes the director will do his own switching. There is no doubt in the minds of anyone but an accountant that the team of a director plus a vision mixer achieves the best results. It is impossible to give equal attention to the content of an interview whilst talking to cameras, working the mixing panel and, most important, lining up the coming items. Add to this the need to pay full attention to the PA, the floor manager and, during live programmes, changes to running orders and timings by the editor, and it is clear that studio direction can be like trying to land a blazing aeroplane whilst listening to a riot going on in air traffic control. If there is a vision mixer, there is no point in the director calling every shot. By the time the words 'camera two' are uttered and the button pressed the moment will have passed. The cuts will all be late.

If the director and vision mixer have confidence in each other it is quite usual for the director to line up the main shots and opening sequence and then let the vision mixer cut an interview on his own initiative. If the vision mixer is inexperienced the director should line up each shot. This does not mean worrying about an exact cutting point. The director has always to think at least one and normally two or three shots ahead.

For example, his talkback might sound like:

'Two-shot on camera three next. Four go into the close shot. Steady four. Three give me the close-up when I cut away. Two get to your closing wide shot. One and four clear to the weather map, etc.'

The vision mixer will take the cuts, with luck, at the precise accurate point. Although the vision mixer is there to carry out the instructions of the director he or she should not cut to a camera which is out of focus, unsteady or shooting off the set even when a director mistakenly calls for the shot.

Whoever actually presses the buttons on the console the same principles which govern picture editing for single camera work apply to studio cutting. Vision mixing is no more or less than instantaneous picture editing.

1 *Listen* to the person who is talking. The director may not be responsible for the editorial content of the interview but the intonation and pace of delivery of a speaker are often clues to a coming cut or change of shot size. It is not impossible to competently direct an interview conducted in an unknown foreign language.

2 *Look* at the ones who are not talking. The commonest difficulty for young directors is learning how to ignore the television transmission monitor which shows what is presently on air. If it's on air, there's not much you can do about it. The director needs to pay attention to the camera monitors which show the choice of next shots. It is a good exercise to switch off the transmission monitor and direct entirely from the row of camera screens. That way the new director can learn to avoid the second commonest problem which is to become so hypnotized by the picture on air that all the remaining cameras, lacking direction, offer up almost identical shots. When the time arrives for a cut there is nothing new to cut to.

3 *Cut* on reactions. Someone eager to join in generally shows it by looks and body movements. The lips begin to move before a sound is uttered. The sharpest cutting is the result of observation and anticipation. Waiting for someone to speak and then deciding to cut

destroys the pace. As with any other kind of conversation the onlooker does not look from A to B on alternate questions and answers as though an interview were a tennis match. It is often more revealing to look at the reactions of the non-speaking party. Creative cutting cannot be learnt from a book. A large part of it is intuitive. If the director's attention instinctively switches from one contributor to another, there is the precise point to cut.

4   *Motivate* the cuts. It is wrong to think that frantically cutting back and forth or randomly changing shot sizes will add excitement to a lacklustre interview. Overcutting just draws attention to dull material. It also can destroy the concentration of the viewers on the subject matter. As sensitive cutting anticipates the precise psychological point where the viewer wants to change the point of view, rapid overcutting virtually implies that the director is seeing the world under the influence of controlled chemical substances. The pace of the interview itself ought to control the rhythm of the cutting, not the artistic pretensions of the director.

5   *Zoom* in vision only when an answer is clearly going to last long enough to cover the entire length of the move. A slow zoom to a closer shot can be effective but needs to be motivated by a heightening of interest or tension. A zoom out is only really effective at the conclusion of an interview or when a guest springs a surprise by producing some object or starts to move agitatedly whilst on camera. It leaves a director with egg all over the face if a slow dramatic zoom to a close-up of a guest is attempted and the guest stops talking before the end of the move. If in doubt the studio director should do as a single camera director does and only change shot size when the subject is out of vision.

6   *Priority* should be given to the guest when shots are being progressively tightened. This means that the shot of the guest should be tightened first and the one of the interviewer to match it second. Conversely at a change of subject or the end of the interview

the shot on the interviewer should be widened first either by a zoom out or a cut from the close-up of the guest to a two-shot.

7   *Avoid* cutting from matching two-shot to two-shot. It may work in television studio drama, particularly with tight over-the-shoulder shots, but cutting between the loose two-shots appropriate to the normal interview often results in apparent jump cuts. This can be comic if the designer has helpfully put a pot plant or the like in the middle of the set. On each cut the flower pot will leap across the screen.

Two and more guests, two and more cameras

Most of what is described above refers to one-plus-one or one-plus-two interviews shot with two or three cameras. These are the likeliest set-ups the beginner is likely to encounter. The rules governing simple interviews are the same as for complex ones as well as studio discussions. Seating plans and cutting will still be dictated by the subject matter and style of programme. The range of shots available will be determined largely by the number of cameras available, as well as the skill of the director in moving them about during the interview. No two interviews or two studio set-ups will ever be identical. A selection of suggested seating arrangements with possible choices of available shots are shown in Appendix A at the back of the book.

5

More boring grammar

Interviews are television at its least complicated. Yet without appreciating the pitfalls and having a basic grasp of television grammar they are stunningly easy to get wrong, either on location or in the studio. Interviews are only the beginning.

Crossing the line

There is nothing harder to explain in words than the grammar of crossing the line of action or the optical barrier as it is often described. There is also nothing easier to demonstrate, by design or by accident. The beginner need not stay awake at night wrestling with the abstract concept since observing a few simple rules can avoid serious trouble. Crossing the line is an unforgivable sin only in the eyes of a complete purist; there are ways of getting away with it when nobody will notice. But every director must be aware at all times of the risks involved. As with most direction problems the root is not the technology of the medium but the psychology of the audience.

The brain is wired to recognize the difference between left and right. Without that we would be perpetually disorientated. The idea comes from the fact that one human can only be in one position looking in one direction at one time. The trouble is that although one person has always the same left and a right there are many different lefts and rights presented by the rest of the world. We stand behind someone and his or her left and right are the same as our own. The person turns to face us. As far as he or she is now concerned our left hand is the other's right hand and vice versa. Left and right are subjective. To illustrate this let us imagine a road in Britain with a bus approaching (we have to specify in Britain because the bus will be on the left-hand side of the road). Person A and person B are facing each other on opposite sides of the

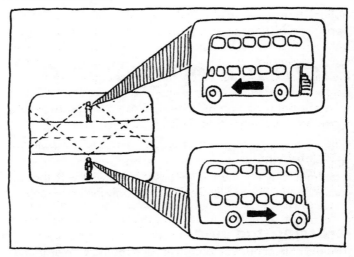

Figure 5.1

road waiting to cross. A looks left at the bus approaching on the far side whilst B looks to the right at the same bus coming on the near side. A recognizes that it is safe to start crossing at least as far as the middle of the road, B can see that it is unwise to step off the pavement until it has passed. There is no problem for the individuals. A sees the action happening from left to right; B sees it from right to left. But let us assume that by some paranormal telepathic process we can suddenly switch their viewpoints between A and B. Person B will perceive the approaching vehicle coming from the left and, on the far side of the road, will happily step off the kerb looking the wrong way, and be promptly mown down.

This is the stuff of nightmares. Unless we are hallucinating we simply cannot do this. But a television director can. Substitute two cameras for person A and B and we have the two opposing viewpoints. So far so good until we start cutting between the two. Now in alternate shots the same bus is travelling first right to left, then left to right, first it is near then it is on the other side of the road. Ultimately it will either pass itself or meet itself in a head-on collision. Too much of this will give the viewer a nervous breakdown. The equivalent effect can easily occur by accident. A simple illustration is a football match. An easy way of shooting a game with two cameras might be to place one on each side of the pitch. Unhappily the cameras will have crossed the optical barrier. The play will be going in diametrically opposite directions on each camera. When the director cuts between them the direction of play reverses at each cut until there is complete visual confusion. Every goal is going to look like an own goal, except the real own goals. Only the colours of the shirts will give the poor viewer the slightest idea of what is going on. In monochrome the game would make no more sense that a disturbed ants' nest.

Helpful hint

A director should always be careful to define which left he or she is talking about. It is good practice to always talk of 'camera left' or 'camera right' both on location and in the television gallery. This is the left and right of the camera lens in question. Similarly in directing performers camera left and right are the terms to use. Stage actors unfortunately are accustomed to think in terms of 'stage left' and 'stage right', i.e. their own left and right hands when they are facing an audience. They also talk of moving 'upstage' when they go back from the camera and 'downstage' when they go towards it. This is because theatre stages traditionally are raked from front to back, not flat like television studio floors. When several actors are in a complicated scene or where multiple cameras are involved it is essential to differentiate between the two in the language of direction. It is quite a simple habit to acquire. 'Three will you crab camera left and follow Sir John. Ask him to move stage right...Two pan camera right for a two shot of the soldiers upstage, ask them both to take a pace stage left...on the drum beat let them leave the shot camera right.'

The humble one-plus-one interview can run into trouble. We have established that the way to shoot this is cross shooting with the cameras as close as possible to the eyelines of the participants. There is an invisible line of action which to all intents passes between the two noses. Any pictures shot within 180° on the same side of the two will look natural. On each cut the two will appear to be looking in each other's direction as in a normal conversation. However, if one camera should stray behind one performer and across to shoot over the far

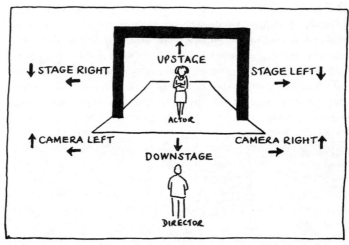

Figure 5.2

shoulder the shots become ridiculous. On each cut the two participants will no longer be facing each other but will seem to be sitting behind each other as if on a bus.

Take this one stage further to the traditional cinema sequence of the *High Noon* style gunfight. So long as the two cameras remain on the same side of the street the two gunslingers will advance closer with every cut. When the bad guy in the black hat draws his pistol only to fall to his knees in a pool of blood we know that the good guy in the white hat has been the faster. Now if the two cameras set up on opposite sides of the street the two gunslingers appear to follow each other along the road and at the moment of truth, with a close-up of the bad guy's hand going for the gun followed by a long shot of the same bad guy falling slain, it will look for all the world as though he has just shot himself in the back. In conclusion, so long as the cameras stay on the same side of the 180° line of action all ought to be well. Up to a point that is. The complication is that the line can keep changing and sometimes there is more than one line!

Let us look at a table-top demonstration. Logic tells us that if there is a line of action the table top is like a football field and that so long as all the cameras stay somewhere within an arc in front of the table all the shots should cut and all will be well. If this was to be nothing but a game of table-top football this would be the case. But the presence of the demonstrator introduces a new line. The demonstrator is talking direct to the viewer. The viewer is one-half of an interview set-up. There is a line of action running between these two noses, the one in vision and the one watching.

This is easier shown on camera than explained simply because the brain has difficulty coping with something which it is conditioned to regard as impossible. Consider a demonstration shot on two cameras. If camera one is the traditional mid-shot 'chat' camera and camera two offers close-ups from either left or right there is no problem. Any two shots will cut. Now introduce a third camera. If the work surface is very cluttered with props the temptation will be to place camera two at one end of the table and camera three at the other.

The shot of the demonstrator on camera one will cut with either of the shots on the other two cameras. But the two other cameras are as surely facing each other as the two people facing each other across the street as the bus approaches. Try to intercut cameras two and three and objects will jump back and forth across the screen, and if the demonstrator comes into successive shots there will be alternate left and right profile shots and the same hand coming once left to right and then right to left. Finally, to add to the confusion, let us introduce a fourth camera to take shots over the shoulder. The images are coming from all four points of the compass. Randomly cut between them and complete confusion is guaranteed. The only sure fire way of keeping out of trouble will be to keep all four cameras within a mere 90° arc of the demonstrator, to one side or the other. The trouble with playing it that safe is whilst television grammar will be maintained it may now be impossible to get all the shots the director wants. So it is going to be inevitable from time to time that the director must be prepared to throw away the rules and find ways to cross the dreaded optical barrier.

What must be clear is:

1   The director does it knowingly, not finding it a horrid shock in the studio or the editing suite.
2   It is done in a way that does not disorientate and annoy the viewer.
3   If it is done as a deliberate effect it should be recognizable as one and not look like the director's mistake.

The same old message. Break all the rules you like but know when and why you are doing it.

Crossing the line can be made to pass unobserved by the viewer.

1   As it is always possible to cut from any of the close-ups, except the over-the-shoulder one, to the mid-shot or long shot of the demonstrator it is always safe to cut this master shot between the close-ups. Although safe this might result in a ping-pong directing style like close-up–mid-shot–close-up–mid-shot–close-up. This should not happen if as a result of the rehearsal the props on the work surface are sensibly grouped so that all the close-ups during one section come all from the same end of the table.

2   The closer the close-up the less worrying the crossing of the line will appear. If something as small as a matchbox fills the screen and a finger tip appears in shot to indicate it, nobody is likely to notice that the hand was moving right to left in the mid-shot but the finger tip reappeared descending left to right in the close-up.

3   The greater the difference the camera angle between the two shots the less any lack of continuity will be noticed. As we will explain the eye and the brain will happily accept cuts of quite contrasting kinds and a cut between a high angle wide shot and a low angle close-up of an object will disguise any incidental line crossing. For this reason the over-the-shoulder shot can be made to work. By its nature it is likely to be both at an exaggerated high angle and offering a big close-up of the action. What would not work would be a mid-shot from the front cut to a similar mid-shot from behind.

Accidental crossing of the line ought to be difficult in any rehearsed studio production simply because any problem should be immediately obvious on the camera monitors. Just switching between cameras will conclusively prove whether cuts will work or not. With single camera work when there are pauses between each set-up and actions are shot out of sequence things can be more tricky. The shooting of reverse-angle questions and cutaways is a case in point. If the eyeline of the interviewer is not the opposite to that of the guest the line will have been crossed. The two will appear to be looking in the same direction with the one talking to the back of the head of the other. Walking shots can be a menace when one is to be cut to another.

If our interview is to start walking in front of a stately home in the first set-up and continue at the stable block in the second one the convention is for the performers to walk through the frame and disappear left or right and for them to reappear moving apparently in the same direction in the following picture. But if the camera crosses the line they will seem to have walked out of shot to the left and immediately returned from the same direction as though they had walked into a wall or remembered they had left something behind. If performers exit camera left normally we expect them to re-enter from camera right.

There are ways of minimizing or disguising the problem.

1   Shots moving from left to right or vice versa will always cut to shots of the performers moving straight towards or away from the camera. These are neutral shots and can be used to reverse a line of action. They are frequently used to bridge left to right and right to left movements in car chases.

2   An extremely high angle shot will establish a new geography and disguise line crossing.

3   Salvation in the editing suite is found in well-chosen cutaway shots. The location director should never return without having made time for shooting as many as possible.

Certain types of studio programme frequently involve line crossing. The sort of debate involving a panel of guests and a large participating studio audience is a case in point. Even with a multiplicity of cameras there are going to be times when the optical barriers are confused. Different lines apply when the guests on the stage debate amongst themselves, the audience argues to and fro, a presenter walks amongst the crowd with a microphone and when the audience and a member of the stage panel have an altercation. So long as there are repeated reminders of the real geography of the set-up, like wide shots of the audience from the stage or a wide angle of the whole studio from the back, the audience will forgive and forget any visual confusion. Nonetheless

Word of warning

Members of the Yoof Pol Pot School of Direction have been heard to dismiss the need to take any notice of line crossing. The arguments are twofold. Repeatedly crossing the line looks like a creative style rather than a mistake, and it is always possible to correct a mistake by flipping the offending image back to front as a simple digital effect during post production.

In other words crossing the line is one of those boring old fashioned problems which can be left to the picture editor to sort out later. Certainly deliberate crossing of optical barriers has a place. In drama it can be used to imply menace or madness. As a stylistic device it works well when cutting many kinds of music. Reversing pictures to restore a visual logic is nothing new. It is done frequently when archive film is assembled. An example is any attempt to illustrate a battle from various sources of newsreel footage. War correspondents are not too fussy about the optical barrier when shells are whistling overhead. But in any compilation one army has to be moving consistently in one direction across the screen and the enemy in the other (except when retreating).

Keeping the material as originally shot would portray an unseemly brawl with both sides shelling themselves or taking turns to attack the same trenches from the same direction. Flipping the image can be a great help when Sod's Law strikes in the editing suite and the best available close-up cutaway of a hand or implement happens to be have been shot from the wrong side of the line of action. It is nonsense though to suggest that technology is going to save the day always at the flick of a switch. Reversing a picture reverses everything. If the scene is in front of Smith's Newsagents prepare for it to be renamed s'htimS in mirror writing. All people have two non-matching profiles usually emphasized by non-symmetrical hair styles. Button holes will leap from side to side and pot plants reposition themselves. It would be an interesting exercise to try an electronic correction to a crass crossing of the optical barrier when the subject has a parrot on his shoulder.

the convention of not crossing the line should be observed as far as possible. If the rules are ignored completely it will soon appear incomprehensible who is talking to whom; members of the panel will be seen talking to the backs of each other's heads or facing in opposite directions and audience shots from alternative sides of the studio will result in a visual anarchy.

Moving cameras

The interview and demonstration set-ups are most easily covered by static cameras. Interviewers, interviewees and demonstrators are normally static. A whole new dimension is added when either the camera or the subjects of the camera become wholly mobile. A camera shot can move in two possible ways. It can physically be transported from place to place to change the picture.

1   It can track, meaning to move physically towards or away from the subject.

2   It can crab, or move sideways normally to follow a move.

3   It can elevate, meaning go up on its camera mount. Also called craning up.

4   It can depress, which is to go down on the mount. Also called craning down.

Or it can appear to move by a lens effect.

1   It can pan, which entails swivelling the camera left or right on a static mounting.

2   It can tilt or swivel up or down.

3   It can zoom, which is an optical lens effect to widen or narrow the angle of view.

How many of these moves can be achieved depends on the mount. A tripod is limited to moving the lens. Any decent pedestal or other studio camera mounting can achieve all of these basic effects. A really good operator will use various combinations of all these moves in combination to achieve the best possible framing of the shots. For example, a zoom from a long shot to a close-up should involve a pan at the same time to adjust the composition. A track-in may involve a simultaneous tilt up with a pan left or right. Shots combining the different elements are known as developing shots. They are best done so subtly that the audience is not aware of their existence. Any feature film or good quality television drama will employ developing shots throughout. It is important for the director of any sort of production though to be quite clear about the difference between the different moves. A zoom can achieve a very similar framing to a track, and craning up can do something similar to a tilt but the actual effects can be very different.

Tracking, crabbing and craning are difficult to do well by the camera operator but are all easy on the eye. We can know what it feels like to walk towards something, or circle around it and we know how to stand up and peer over a wall. Because the camera reproduces something like normal every day experience there is only confusion if the moves themselves are not sensible. Some directors have a fatal fascination with 360° tracking shots around a performer which serve no apparent purpose at all. Hunting hyenas may circle their prey but such behaviour at a party might draw attention to itself. American television directors seem to lump together each of these different camera moves as a 'dolly'. The main moving camera problems arise with panning, tilting and zooming.

The pan

The human head can pan, but the eyes can not. Eyes can only cut. The point is easily proved. Watch anyone looking out of the window of a moving train. Rather than keep a fixed stare as the landscape pans past, the eyes constantly flicker side to side, taking a series of rapid snapshots. When a head pans across a landscape the eye flickers from point of interest to point of interest as the eye and brain select and focus on them. One of the big differences in the experience of going to the cinema and watching on a normal domestic television is that the cinema screen is large enough for the eye to flit around wide-angle shots and select points of interest. The small scale and low quality domestic TV set does not allow this luxury. In consequence the television pan is an unnatural move. It works painlessly though if well done. That means using it to reveal new visual information and allow the viewer to interpret the move as a series of mental cuts.

1   If a pan is too fast it confuses the eye. The very fast 'whip pan' reduces the image to a blur. This can be

used as a deliberate dramatic effect. A normal pan done too fast can produce a strobing effect on the television screen, particularly in the case of close-ups and shots with a high contrast between the back and foregrounds. On older generation video cameras there can even be a smearing effect on the picture.

2   If a pan is too slow it becomes dreary. If there is not new information revealed at a comfortable rate and the eye has nothing new to stimulate it there is a subconscious urge to cry out 'get on with it will you!' Unless the subject is the limitless tedium of the Empty Quarter or the Siberian wastes the slow pan is to be treated with caution.

3   There is no point of a pan from one subject to another if there is nothing informative in between. If the background in the middle of a pan is irrelevant or distracting it is better to do what the eye does and cut straight from A to B.

4   A pan has to have a beginning and an end. If the camera starts to pan it will automatically be assumed that it is doing so to reveal something of great interest. If it goes nowhere in particular but comes to rest just because the operator cannot find anything more interesting to focus on the viewer might want to ask if the journey was really necessary.

Tilting up and down raises the same problems though normally in less acute ways. A tilt up is one way of approximating the way we appraise each other to take in status, and particularly sexual attraction. (Men and women do size each other up in a predictable series of anatomical 'shots' though they do not invariably start at the ankles and progressively move to the face or vice versa.) A tilt is a good way of giving the impression of grandeur in the case of a towering building or forest tree. Because of the incompatibility of vertical human proportions and the oblong television screen the pan up or down may be the only available way to portray subjects like models in fashion shows.

The zoom

Neither the eyes nor the brain can zoom. The zoom was never intended to be used as an optical effect but was a device for combining the possibilities of a whole range of fixed angle lenses in a single optical unit. Even then it was never welcomed by serious film cinematographers who continue in most cases to prefer fixed lenses. Technical design problems of video cameras rather than artistic requirements gave the zoom its dominance. Zooming in vision is a dramatic effect which tends to draw attention to itself. So it is either best deliberately used for that purpose or avoided. The distinguishing mark of amateur home movies is the incessant use of the zoom, generally combined with endless and aimless pans.

A zoom is not the same as a track. With a track-in the angle of view remains constant and as the camera moves, any foreground passes on either side and the background simultaneously changes perspective to reveal or conceal visual information. A zoom simply changes the angle of view, selecting a part of a picture and dragging it towards the viewer (or the reverse). There is not often an excuse for showing a zoom in a properly equipped studio. It is most noticeable in very low budget talk shows and is more to do with the disinclination of the camera operators to move from one spot than the creativity of the director.

A location unit with a single camera and a tripod may have no alternative to using the zoom to follow action. The question must always be asked whether it is necessary to show the zoom movement or whether cuts between static frames will do the job more neatly. Zooms, combined with other moves are common in developing shots which are part and parcel of filming drama. The essence is that they should be completely unobtrusive to the audience and used as a subtle way to tighten or loosen shots. Once they become obvious the suspension of disbelief that naturalistic drama depends on can be shattered.

Since the zoom is a visual trick it is something easily done as a digital video effect in post production. It is also susceptible to all sorts of fun and games. Zooming in and simultaneously tracking out, or vice versa, in an amusing trick much copied since Stephen Spielberg's film *Jaws*. The subject remains the same size in the frame whilst the background appears to zoom. To get the timing right the director must allow for interminable takes and get a very patient camera operator.

Moving people

As cameras and lenses can move in relation to performers so the performers can move in relation to cameras. The director now has a range of new problems to consider before selecting a lens angle and a camera position. Just as the choice of an angle of view can change the perspective and appearance of static characters in a landscape so a similar choice can affect the impression of speed and excitement once the subjects begin to move.

Recall the main considerations for setting up a static shot:

1   Camera position in relation to the subject
2   Camera height and angle of view
3   Lens angle and depth of field
4   Whether successive shots will cut

Now consider the possibility of the performer no longer static but coming towards the camera or moving across the frame from side to side.

The narrower the angle of view the less the depth of field. So if a performer or vehicle comes directly towards the lens he or it will rapidly pass in and out of focus. If the subject is going to stay sharply defined the camera operator will have to 'pull focus', i.e. constantly adjust the focus throughout the length of the walk. This is a measure of a good cameraman. Even so pulling focus is not something to be done unrehearsed and is only reliably done if the camera operator has an assistant to manipulate the focus ring during the move. Matters are even more complicated with a long walk towards camera as the operator will have to adjust the framing by subtle tilting and zooming at the same time. However, the move towards the narrow-angle lens creates some interesting effects. Since both foreground and background will be mostly out of focus the viewer will have very little reference to the speed of the approach. At the furthest end of a telephoto lens the resulting shot can resemble slow motion.

A shot often seen is of an aeroplane taking off filmed from the end of a runway. For obvious reasons the director will prefer to be as far back as possible, and to frame the plane from its starting position the camera will be low down. The foreground will be partly out of focus and distorted by heat haze and aviation fuel fumes from the tarmac. As the aeroplane takes off it will be thundering towards the camera at several hundred miles an hour but will appear quite differently. The relative increase in size in the frame from start to finish will develop incredibly slowly. Without other points of reference in focus the aircraft will seem almost to hover until the final moments when it fills the frame or rises overhead.

A similar popular shot is of a crowd from a high vantage point on the narrowest angle lens. On a static shot the crowd pass in and out of focus as a sea of bobbing heads. When the intention is to follow one figure in the crowd the operator has to follow focus and adjust the framing to hold the subject sharp whilst the swirling movement around moves in and out of a blurred fore- and background. There is a dreamlike effect created.

There is yet another complication to introduce. Depth of field also depends on the amount of light available. The smaller a camera aperture the greater the depth of field, but also the greater amount of light needed to record the image. The aircraft and crowd scenes described will need a reasonable depth of field if the cameraman is to have any chance of holding focus. So the best bet is to choose a bright sunny day. Conversely there could be too much light around to create the desired mood. A sharply defined background may be the last thing desired. In which case there has to be an alternative means of reducing the light and enabling the camera to use a very small aperture. Video cameras come with what are called neutral density filters built in, film cameras have a matte box which is a filter holder in front of the lens. Using neutral density (ND) filters the operator can effectively put sun glasses on the camera.

Shooting an approaching subject on a long lens seems to slow things down. Shooting on a wide-angle lens has precisely the opposite effect. In this case our camera on the runway will portray the aircraft as a merest dot on the horizon. The perspective drawing of the runway will be such as to appear filling the full width of the frame in the foreground and narrowing to a point of infinity. The impression is increased by the tapering of the two straight, parallel sides and possibly navigation lights along the middle. Everything will be in sharp focus. As the plane takes off it will appear to travel even faster than in reality, it will start as a dot and end by filling the entire picture. A runway is not the most opportune place to try this as on a wide angle the camera might have to be placed uncomfortably close to the approaching aircraft, but this wide-angle shot is particularly popular for filming railways. The trains appearing to race towards the camera and finish either roaring past or even passing overhead. If safety regulations allow, half bury a camera in the shingle between the sleepers or alongside the track. Do not expect the camera operator to stay with it.

Car chases gain a lot of excitement from wide-angle shots combined with low camera positions. A car approaching at 20 miles per hour can appear to be travelling at 70. A crash or accident can be portrayed by cutting just as the approaching vehicle fills the wide-angle frame and dubbing suitable sound effects.

> **Trick of the trade**
> It may be intended that the approaching vehicle comes to a shuddering halt at the point of filling the frame with a number plate or radiator grill. No operator will welcome the idea of sitting in the middle of the road even if a professional stunt driver is in charge. The safe option would be to stay well back from the marked stopping point and use a narrow-angle lens, but this ruins the impression of speed which demands the wide angle. An easy solution is to start with the camera on its widest angle close up on the number plate and for the vehicle to reverse as fast as possible out of shot. The tape can then be reversed in post production. Do not try this on the public highway and make sure the driver is familiar with the gearbox.

So much for performers and vehicles coming towards narrow- or wide-angle lenses. If the action is across the screen the reverse conditions apply. Anything going across the screen on a wide angle seems slowed down. Anything going across the screen on a narrow-angle lens seems speeded up.

On a wide angle a figure only a dozen or so metres away will appear as a small figure taking ages to cross a wide horizon. This can be a very useful shot because of the depth of field involved. A shot could start with a vast but clearly defined panorama of desert or jungle which a presenter, physically close to the camera position, can enter whilst holding forth, cross frame slowly and exit without the audience's attention ever wavering from the geography. But if the performer were to run across the shot for dramatic reasons the effect would be very tame.

Contrariwise our runner shot running across frame from a distant camera position on a narrow-angle lens appears to be travelling amazingly fast. To hold the shot the camera will have to pan with the performer. Because of the angle any background will pass through shot at great speed. Psychologically we judge speed forward by the apparent reverse speed of a background. Remember the disorientation you feel when sitting in a stationary railway carriage and another train alongside starts to pull away. There is a sudden panic-inducing sensation that it is the stationary carriage which is on the move. The impression will be heightened because not only will the background to our runner be racing past but it will also appear as an out-of-focus blur.

Shooting a static or slowly walking performer on the narrow-angle end of the lens through foreground activity can be used to convey an impression of a busy environment. Much of the background will remain in distant focus but any foreground activity will rush through shot as a blur. Shooting performers across a busy street with passing crowds and foreground buses can create a great impression of frantic activity. The more complex the shot the greater the potential problems for the camera and, just as important, for the sound. The 'how do you see it?' type of ignorant director who leaves everything to the camera crew is matched by the know-all who insists on shots that are plainly impossible for the conditions and time available. At the end of the day the director is the boss, but camera crews merit consideration and consultation.

A careful choice of shots can bring quality to the most mundane story and immediately distinguishes the professional director from the slapdash one.

Helpful hint

When working with an inexperienced camera operator it can pay to check picture composition. A natural cameraman like a natural photographer should have an instinctive eye for composition but it doesn't pay to bet on it. A lot of location camera operators these days are untrained ex-despatch riders. A face or a figure should always show what is called 'looking room'.

In any composition there should be more empty space in front of the head than behind and the more profile the shot the greater the looking room. If looking room is not provided and the nose of the subject is closer to the edge of the screen than the other the picture is annoying.

If two such compositions are cut together in an interview there is an instant impression of them banging their noses together. Looking room is essential in any walking shots. A walking shot makes the viewer want to keep ahead of the character and anticipate what is to be revealed, not to look back at what has already been passed. It is the anticipation or curiosity of the viewer which gives motivation to a moving or developing shot. Just as instinctively a viewer wants to see both eyes of someone talking so they need to share the point of view of someone physically moving or looking from A to B. A camera operator offering incompetently framed shots might be cured by the John Grierson treatment of a stretch in the National Portrait Gallery but is probably better off with a career delivering pizzas.

Canted angles and other obsessions

Some directors seem to show a peculiar penchant for employing one-legged camera operators or two-legged tripods. They strain for effect by abandoning natural horizons in favour of canting the camera angle 45° or so to the left or right. The impression given is of a camera tripod on deck during the last hours of the *Titanic*. The effect if used is exaggerated in combination with walking/talking presentation and low wide angles. This effect can be created digitally in post production but is a favourite of certain hand-held camera operators who attempt to cover interviews from a kneeling position between the performers and have never heard of picture editing. An older description of Canted Angle is 'Dutch Angle' as in 'Dutch Take' or 'Dutch Courage'.

Canted angles are almost as old as the cinema and were used with particular dramatic effect by Orson Welles amongst many other directors. The classic Carol Reed film *The Third Man* has lengthy sequences shot at canted angles to convey mystery, tension or terror. Anyone who thinks that using them is a creative breakthrough or a revolutionary style should go home and work on a blueprint for the wheel. Because canted camera angles are deliberately unnatural and disorientating they should be used with that in mind. As with aggressive and repeated pans and zooms they are often the mark of inept home videos rather than properly directed stories. If a style makes it difficult to distinguish pretentiousness from incompetence the director needs to examine his or her motives for choosing it.

Canted shots do have their uses. As always the great exception is shooting music. A montage sequence of shop fronts or street signs and skyscrapers, particularly at night, is exciting from low canted angles. This is not unnatural. A passer-by in London's Piccadilly Circus looks up and tilts the head to read the neon advertisements. It is impossible to look up in Manhattan without seeing canted angles. If these pictures are to be cut in sequence together it is important to alternate the right and left angles otherwise they will appear as jump cuts.

A point of view shot from a toddler on the floor to towering adults can be represented by a canted angle as can a view from a hospital bed or a dentist's chair. It fairly represents the points of view of an audience at a fashion show looking up at a catwalk. Canted angles add little to a picture of a presenter walking down a street, a politician making a speech or an interview in a restaurant. Nor do they automatically make presenters look more fascinating, beautiful or exciting.

6

Here's one I prepared earlier

Directing demonstrations

If the commonest set-up in broadcast television is the interview, the second most familiar is the demonstration.

A television demonstration is any programme item where a presenter or expert practitioner explains and performs some process directly to the audience. This may be wrapped up to look like an interview. A guest of a show can perform the demonstration whilst a regular anchor person remains on the set to pose questions and chivvy along the performance. There is a small risk that this can complicate the matter of eyelines. Is the demonstrator addressing the anchor person or the viewer? Whatever the chosen style of packaging the demonstration is a performance for the camera. During an interview the members of the audience are silent witnesses or eavesdroppers. In a demonstration the viewer is down in the front row of the stalls watching the show.

Demonstrations crop up almost anywhere but are particularly important in children's television, programmes on science and technology and breakfast and daytime magazine programmes. Non-broadcast training videos are often demonstrations pure and simple. Gardening and cookery programmes are all based around demonstrations. A demonstration can encompass pretty well any scale of activity from how to keep fit to how to dock an aircraft carrier or fold paper napkins.

The problem with directing all of them is how to show both whatever the demonstrator is doing whilst simultaneously illustrating the explanation with close-up details which the viewer otherwise would miss. In other words the problem is going to be one of continuity. Continuity is a particular problem for the single camera director.

The obvious place to conduct most demonstrations is the multi camera studio. One camera can concentrate on the presenter in a wide-angle shot and the others will be available for close-ups of hands at work, the objects described and the processes involved. Many multi camera demonstrations can be arranged to take place in real time so the whole thing will fit a pre-arranged duration and can be shot in one continuous take. The best of both worlds is achieved by doing demonstrations on an outside broadcast. This is the medium of choice for demonstrations which demand the great outdoors such as training sheep dogs or programmes on gardening. Despite this the economics of production will usually mean that the entire programme or series will have to be based on the use of the outside broadcast scanner. A studio on wheels is an expensive piece of kit and is unlikely to be affordable for five minute demonstration items for a magazine programme. The likely choice then is either to use the studio or shoot on a single camera.

There are good reasons why many demonstrations cannot be brought into the studio, and because of these every director must know the tricks of the trade for covering them with a single camera.

Scale

The largest object that can get in to most television studios is about the size of a small car. You are unlikely to be able to demonstrate a combine harvester in a studio. You can show how to take geranium cuttings but not how to fell an oak tree. Even an outside broadcast multi camera set-up can lose out to the single camera in some instances. If the scale of the process is huge and demands numerous set-ups, each to be individually lit, shot and subsequently edited together, the outside broadcast director may come close to shooting each set-up with one camera at a time anyhow. At the other end of the scale a demonstration may need extreme close-up or even microscopic shooting which is best left to the single camera with specialist lenses.

Lighting

Studio lighting generally requires the presenter to work towards the cameras in only one direction. This is fine for cookery but not so helpful for processes which can only be demonstrated in the round and when solutions like using a turntable are not appropriate. It is quicker and simpler to relight between set-ups with location lights.

Time scale

Studio and outside broadcast productions score when a demonstration is of a finite length and when the outcome is predictable. Any process which takes place over a long period of time will need editing. Any process which is technically complex for either the demonstrator or the cameras may necessitate a large number of retakes and a lot of post production work. Single camera shooting may be more flexible and cheaper.

Presentation

Most people can manage to present quite laudable demonstrations to camera in a studio. People who are normally retiring can blossom when asked to show their skill at something they know and love best. Those who would freeze like a rabbit in car headlights if asked to read an autocue can chatter fluently to camera when describing something they are doing with their hands. A decent researcher or producer will look out for natural performers. The problems arise where there is one expert alone who can demonstrate and he or she is incapable of a continuous television performance. In this case the choice of a less stressful single camera set-up and the possibility of multiple retakes is one answer.

> ### Words of warning
> Anything involving smoke, flames, volatile chemicals or even significant amounts of water does not belong in the electronic studio. Even a simple bale of hay may be counted a significant safety hazard. Health and safety regulations are very tight and rightly so. Television can be a very dangerous business. No producer or director should bring any demonstration more risky than needlework to a studio without checking first all the safety considerations. Many locations for demonstrations take place in industrial or technical areas. Hospitals and laboratories may specify protective clothing. Industrial sites may demand ear defenders, protective footwear, hard hats or safety goggles. Even farms may require wellington boots for the crew to pass through disinfectant dips. It is the job of the director to establish any problems, warn the crew and make any necessary arrangements.

A location demonstration is not something to be improvised. The director ought to follow through a sequence of procedures if there is not going to be fear and loathing when the crew arrives on the shooting day.

Research

Unless the director has complete confidence in the calibre of research he ought not to rely exclusively on the reports of researchers or producers. The director must always try to visit the proposed location, meet the demonstrator, and ideally observe the intended demonstration in person. It is likely that the demonstrator will have had no previous television experience. Non-professionals often have the greatest difficulty understanding that something they have done a hundred times the same way may have to be modified and restructured for the camera. Few have any idea of screen time. Asked over the telephone how long something takes they are likely to say confidently 'oh, about ten minutes' and then find that it takes thirty on television.

It is quite usual to arrive somewhere like a laboratory to find the chosen presenter working at a bench against a wall where the demonstration would be impossible to light and the only available camera shot is the back of the presenter's head. The amateur cook very likely works normally against a brilliantly lit window with his or her back to the room. Without considerable rearrangement the only possible shots would be from the middle of the flower bed outside. The director will need firmness and tact if there is not to be the howl of despair, 'But that's the way I always do it!' The whole exercise may sometimes have to be moved somewhere else, another room or even the house next door. There is no point in hoping that the camera crew will be able to solve these sorts of problems on the day.

The commonest difficulty, and the one hardest to resolve, is space. The demonstration area has to have room not just for the crew but for the tripod, which is surprisingly space consuming, and the lights. Lighting stands eat up space. The work area has to be brought well forward from any wall to avoid shadows and allow backlighting. Some very tight cutaways may be impossible to shoot on the main location and may have to be mocked up and repeated somewhere else. Standard lighting may not suit the occasion. Very close-up shooting may require small fresnel lens spotlights; a whole laboratory might require extra floodlights. The camera crew needs to have all this information in advance and it is the job of the director to provide it.

A shooting script

A demonstration is close to drama and the director ought to be clear about what is going to happen and in what sequence it is going to be shot. It may be that the demonstration will be broken down into sequences different from the order in which they will be edited together. Close-ups will always be shot separately and in the order most convenient for the lighting set-up. If a demonstration opens with a shot of a hand picking up a spanner and ends with a hand putting the spanner down, the director will shoot the two spanner close-ups at the same time and then go to light the other close-up shots also out of sequence. This makes it very easy to forget key shots in the heat of the moment. The pigeons come to roost in the edit suite.

Demonstrations follow a logical narrative from beginning to end. If the whole thing is to be intelligible the viewer must be able to follow the process step by step. If part of the demonstration is not shown the frustration of the viewer will be immediate. If the demonstrator says 'and as you see, as I add the solution the litmus paper turns slowly blue' and the director has forgotten the shot, there is no way out. To avoid this the director ought to work out a list of the absolutely necessary key shots decided as a result of the recce. The director can tick them off as the shoot progresses and use them as a checklist with the camera operator.

This has become increasingly important as it is no longer normal, as once it was, for a PA to attend location shoots to keep continuity. Drawing up a detailed written list of essential shots may not be the only or the most efficient kind of aide-mémoire. A storyboard can be even more successful particularly when continuity depends on remembering which actions were performed by the left hand and which by the right.

Rehearsal

Wherever possible the director should have seen a dry run of the demonstration during the recce and agreed with the demonstrator how to shorten or enlarge certain sequences, which demonstration areas are to be used, and what equipment or props will be needed on the day. The first thing to do when the crew arrives is to perform a complete run-through. This could be a total rehearsal with speech or might have to be a descriptive mime. '...I put the thing into the centrifuge here with this hand and then when the dial goes into the red here I pick up the other sample with this hand like this and talk about what is happening...'

Precise timing is less important on location than in the studio as almost any demonstration can be shortened easily in the editing, assuming of course that the director got all the shots in the first place. The rehearsal tells the camera operator what he needs to know about the lights and is a final check for the director that all the shots that will be needed are listed or correctly storyboarded. A good operator will probably be able to suggest alternative set-ups and additional close shots. The director can rarely have too many of the latter.

Equipment and properties

The provision of extra props and equipment may be the agreed responsibility of the demonstrator or it may be the job of the director. All demonstrations tend to consume materials and single camera ones, with the likelihood of multiple retakes, consume most of all. For example, the demonstration may be as simple as how to make an omelette. The director has to check that there is a large surplus of eggs and other ingredients. It makes no sense to have to stop for a panic visit to the village shop. With many demonstrations last minute replacement materials may not be obtainable at all. Once upon a time a director might have had the services of a stage manager or assistant floor manager to assist on difficult demonstrations. Today, a director must provide for himself.

A good operative should come with a basic tool kit of various useful items like a Swiss Army knife, double-sided tape, spray adhesive, blu-tack, thumb tacks, staples, coloured chalks, fishing line, marking tape and tissues, J-cloths and a bowl for clearing up. A little powder for the sweating lip or shining pate is useful. Each item can help save the day when shooting demonstrations, and the resourceful modern director obliged to work solo will need to build up his own personal selection.

It is particularly useful to go on location with a selection of black or grey velvet drapes. They are invaluable for covering windows, curing reflections and concealing obtrusive furnishings. You need a roll of strong gaffer tape to hold them up.

Stopping points

If the subject is appropriate, the demonstration should be broken down into a number of sequences for shooting purposes. Ideally the process would be shot continuously once in a wide shot to cover the entire action, and then repeated exactly once or twice more for the mid-shots and close-ups. This may not be always possible. If the demonstration area is large and involves more than one lighting set-up there will have to be recording breaks. There are subjects which can be shot once only. Retakes for close-up shots may be out of the question. If there is a demonstration of a new kind of fire extinguisher you cannot set fire to the same car twice, unless you are shooting a Hollywood epic or a commercial with a monstrous budget. You cannot repeat a demonstration of a haircut. There will have to be planned stops to halt and shoot the appropriate close-ups and cutaways before proceeding.

Continuity of action

A demonstration is a piece of drama and the job of the director is to supply the picture editor with shots that will edit together seamlessly. The first requisite is the shooting script or storyboard which ensures that an adequate number of shots are supplied. This alone does not guarantee that the shots will work when the time comes to stitch them together. In many demonstrations the performer, together with the hands, is constantly in shot. It is very difficult to repeat exactly the same gestures at exactly the same speed. The editor can have the greatest difficulty finding a cutting point which does not look like a jump cut or involve a double action.

The answer is to overlap all action. For example, in a wide shot a cook may pick up a glass of wine, add some to a saucepan and then put it down again. To cover this in the close-ups the shot should begin with the glass on the table, the hand should come into frame, take hold of it, and then take it out of frame. It is as well to repeat the entire action more than once and at slightly different speeds. Close-ups often have to be performed at artificially contrived slow speeds to have time to register on the screen. The slow motion actually looks more natural in some cases. The director, with an eagle eye for continuity, should next repeat the action for the setting down of the glass starting with the bare table and letting the hand drop into the shot, position the glass and then withdraw the hand, remembering that there will be less wine in the glass when it is put down than when it was picked up. This will give the editor a wide choice of points to cut during the movement to match the action in the wide shot. A common fault is for the director to ignore action and shoot a series of static cutaway shots as though a demonstration was no different to a banal news report. In the example above it would be simple to shoot a couple of straight cutaways of wine glasses on a table. The shots would be useless as at no vital point would they relate to the actions of the demonstrator. The advice is never to think of demonstration close-ups as mere cutaways. Each and every shot is an integral part of the story narrative. This is not to say that there can be no real cutaways. For example, if our cook is kneading dough for a pizza a repetitive tight shot will be tedious. A cutaway mid close-up of the chef's face and shoulder movements can easily be dropped in to shorten the process. This sort of cutaway is one that is useful even in recorded multi camera studio demonstrations if some editing is envisaged. One advantage of showing an anchor person alongside the demonstrator is the possibility of using reaction shots as cutaways.

Helpful hint

Editing tape in a linear system will be speeded up if the master wide shots are recorded on one cassette and the tight shots and cutaways on another. A great deal of shot searching and tape spooling can be avoided.

Continuity of sound

Most demonstrations involve continuous spoken commentary by the demonstrator. Demonstrations are best unscripted and spontaneous so exactly the same dialogue cannot be expected twice. It can be helpful to get an approximation of delivery and timing by asking the demonstrator to repeat bits of narrative whilst performing the close-up shots. It will help get the pace of the performance right and may give the picture editor an alternative set of sound edits. Sound is free. Always shoot good sound. The statement 'don't bother about microphones this is just a mute cutaway' is thoroughly dangerous. Close-up shots demand close-up sound. If our cook clinks two wine glasses together in close-up and we do not hear the sound on the screen the shot will seem peculiarly unreal. Story editors waste months of their working lives trying to dub on sound effects which ought to have been recorded at the time.

Trick of the trade

If a demonstration can be covered in a continuous wide shot and the close-up shots repeated in sequence immediately afterwards it is very helpful if the demonstrator can match the close-up actions to the original words. It helps if the director makes a sound recording on a cassette machine during the main take and then asks the demonstrator to repeat the actions to playback. This is not foolproof. Sound recording alone will help recapitulate which close-ups will be needed and give an idea of timing but it will not inform the director how the actions were performed, whether by the left hand or the right hand or whether an object was on a work top or being held aloft at a given moment. It is possible to rewind and play back a recording through the viewfinder of most cameras but this can be irksome to watch by more than one or two people at a time. If the demonstration is of an archaeological type and the presenter is working in a trench it is not practical to keep stopping, rewinding, and leaping in and out of the setting. A better solution is to take a separate playback machine and a good size television monitor to the location. The master recording can then be played back to the demonstrator who can watch the original performance, and simultaneously repeat exactly the same gestures for the close-up shots.

Demonstrations in the studio

The multi camera studio or outside broadcast is the ideal choice for shooting the great majority of demonstrations. Most of them benefit from the controlled studio situation, require only a simple setting and can be completed in a finite period of time. There are none of the location problems of shooting in cramped conditions. So long as all the action can be presented in a single direction towards the cameras the lighting problems are unlikely to be difficult. Well-planned and executed demonstrations combine information and entertainment in equal measure. They are very suitable for live transmission. Simple ones involving hobby subjects like flower arranging or craft work can easily be stretched or cut short to fit the available running time which can be a boon to the director of a live magazine show. Many demonstrators are amateur enthusiasts which in the eyes of a company executive reads dirt cheap. It is no wonder that studio demonstrations have such a perennial all-round popularity.

Almost no other kind of programme is so likely to collapse in a hilarious shambles when things go wrong. A director and interviewer can busk their way through the most tedious and ill-planned interview. The audience will blame first the guest for being a bore or a fool. With a demonstration the desperation of the director is immediately apparent on screen. A live demonstration that starts to go wrong rapidly becomes impossible to save. Catastrophe follows catastrophe. Which is another reason for their allure for viewers. They provide invaluable material for the 'All Right on the Night' type shows made by compiling comic out-takes.

With the exception of demonstrations such as keep fit, which demands a large studio floor area, the majority can be confined to a small work surface. This is economical on lighting and ensures that the demonstrator is fixed in a single spot. Such simple set-ups seem to be foolproof. As usual they are not. The single camera director should have the benefit of a thorough recce, and discussions about the demonstration before ever booking the camera crew. There should be no major surprises on the shooting day. An outside broadcast director must make time for a recce. Together with the lighting engineer he will have to be fully prepared before anyone can start rigging cameras and lamps.

The studio director starts with a handicap. The

demonstration has frequently been set up by a researcher or producer with a fairly dim concept of what the director needs to know and what the demonstrator needs to be told. There ought to be the possibility of a telephone briefing a day or more before the transmission or recording day but this may not be so. The director and demonstrator may meet for the first time on the fateful day and the director will have to think on his or her feet.

Ideally the item should still be rehearsed as fully as time allows. If possible this should be done away from the studio but with any assigned floor manager or assistant stage manager in attendance. Studio camera time is a very expensive commodity and it is not necessary to waste the time of an entire crew watching a rehearsal. A rehearsal may be possible some time before the studio day which will enable the director to give concrete information about lighting or sound difficulties at a technical planning meeting. More likely there will be a roughly set and lit 'kitchen set' or 'demonstration area' and the fine tuning will have to wait until the recording day. The rehearsal is the place to take timings. There is no point in showing an expert demonstration performed at top speed if the actions allow no time for the cameras to get the shots or the audience to absorb what is going on. The demonstrator will have to be slowed down. Then decisions will have to be made about how sequences can be cut to get the show back within the time slot allocated.

If the show is going out live this is the moment to go through the meaning of the floor manager's signals. Timings can go awry and the presenter may have to speed up or stretch the performance and ad lib for a bit. Most people can do this. But their faces are a wondrous sight if they are faced by a deranged floor manager stretching his arms wide apart and silently mouthing St..r..e..tch when they have no idea what all this means.

> **Words of warning**
> A demonstrator may airily say things like, 'at this point I open the tin of sardines'. Do not be deceived. Opening a tin of sardines can turn into a bloodbath if the tin opener is an unfamiliar design or the act has to be performed at an awkward angle for the cameras. Try it yourself before trusting the optimism of the demonstrator and have someone standing by with a tin of sticking plasters.

The rehearsal, however brief, must establish certain things:

1   *The geography of the performance.* An amateur demonstrator will not be familiar with the studio layout. During any outside rehearsal substitute tables and work surfaces should be laid out as closely as possible to the way they will be on the show.

2   *The layout of the props.* The objects will have to be laid out in a logical sequence so that the demonstrator does not have to reach backwards and forwards at random as might normally happen.

3   *The main camera position.* A professional presenter might be capable of turning to talk to different cameras at arranged points in the direction. An amateur should never be asked to do this. The demonstrator should talk direct to the lens of one camera only and should be clear which one it is. The eyeline should only change when the demonstrator looks towards one of the props involved or is interrupted by an anchor person.

4   *The presentation of objects.* The director should anticipate the problems of the cameras and watch how props are handled and introduced. Demonstrators should minimize the times they pick up objects. They are unlikely to hold them in exactly the same position twice running and if the hands wave about the cameras may be unable to find or focus the shots. It is better to leave objects in prepared positions on the work surface and show them by tilting them towards camera. If it is essential to lift something its position should be pre-arranged, e.g. held at chest height firmly in both hands.

5   *The logic of the performance.* The commentary should lead the cameras in a logical way. For example, an item on house plants might proceed in this sequence:

(a)   Introduction of plant LS or MS demonstrator with plant.

(b)   Description of plant. CU plant in pot. Possibly slow pan bottom to top.

(c)   Details of problem. BCUs yellow leaves, greenfly damage, etc.

If the script goes 'greenfly problems like these...big

houseplants...sometimes at the top but usually at the bottom here...you can see how the whole plant is affected...', etc. the cameras will get very confused.

6   *The phrasing of the commentary.* It is tempting for a demonstrator to start telling the viewers what they ought to be looking at '...now as you can see clearly at this point...' is a dangerous statement in a live performance. If the direction is efficient the close-up will be already up on the screen. But if the camera misses the shot and the audience can see nothing of the sort it will be mightily irritated.

Work surfaces

Demonstrators may be used to working at tables or benches which are ideal for them but quite unsuitable for getting the appropriate shots on camera. Demonstrators also come in all heights and sizes, something which cannot be ascertained over the telephone. A tall presenter with a low work surface can create very unattractive close-up shots if the background to each becomes his or her crotch. So a work surface must be adjustable. More often than not it will have to be raised on blocks and these must be readily at hand. Studio camera pedestals have a limit to how low they can go. In some instances, looking at the gearbox on a motor cycle, for example, it might be an advantage to raise the whole demonstration area on rostra. The available tables should never be taken for granted. The one selected has to be wide enough to take all the materials and equipment required but not so large as to dwarf the demonstrator or impede the cameras from getting in close. The worktop is important for both lighting and sound. A hard and reflective Formica surface could create difficulties for both. Beware of the overenthusiastic designer. It may be very imaginative to evoke a French bistro in a kitchen set by covering the table in check gingham cloth. The result in the close-ups will be visual clutter and confusion. A plain neutral colour will allow items to be seen to their best advantage.

Setting the props

The rehearsal time should be used to decide which materials are needed and in which sequence the demonstrator will call on them. There has to be a compromise between placing the props where the demonstrator works most comfortably, and where the director would best like to put them for the cameras. To stay with our cook, it is likely that he or she would normally work with the ingredients, whisks, scales and so on in a random looking circle all within comfortable reach.

The director though would like these arranged in an aesthetically pleasing composition and the cameras will want them in a logical sequence. It will be hopeless for the cook to say 'the two most important ingredients are the mackerel and the gooseberries' if the mackerel is on the far right and the gooseberries on the left and they both have to be shot on the same camera. Even worse the bowl of fruit might mask the plate of fish. The ingredients should be laid out in a logical order dictated mainly by the sequence in which they are to be introduced. When the positions are agreed the key spots on the work surface should be marked. The cameras can be thrown completely if a repeatedly used object like an electric whisk is lifted from the arranged spot and then at one point carelessly put down somewhere completely different.

One inherent problem in directing with several cameras is that the demonstrator will have to remember to work towards the cameras. This usually means working in the reverse way to normal practice. It is logical in a kitchen to place small ingredients close to hand and large objects further away. In the studio this will mean the larger objects would block the shots of the smaller ones. A chef whisking an omelette will probably hold the bowl tilted towards the body. This will place the egg mixture tilted away from the camera and hidden in shadow. The chef must be persuaded to tilt the bowl towards the lens. A really experienced demonstrator can be told which cameras will be taking which close-ups and will cooperate by tilting things towards the appropriate lens. If a monitor is placed beneath or alongside the main 'chat' camera it can be very helpful for a professional to pace the commentary. This ought not to be tried with amateurs. There is too great a risk of eyes nervously swivelling about from camera lens to monitor and back. An additional confusion can be that a monitor gives a true image, not a mirror image. We are perversely used to watching ourselves in a mirror and compensating for the reversal of left and right. Attempting to use a monitor as a mirror can upset those unfamiliar with the phenomenon.

> **Handy hint**
> Always be sure to note if the demonstrator is left or right handed. It is easy to overlook this even in rehearsal. The lights and set will probably be arranged with a right-handed contributor in mind in the absence of information to the contrary. Getting this wrong may result in the need to rewrite the lighting plot and reverse the setting of the props and may require a change of microphone position. If the demonstration has a subject like calligraphy which by its nature can be shot from one side only, the other only seeing the back of a hand, the director is well and truly stuffed. The ideal demonstrator would be Leonardo Da Vinci who was both ambidextrous and could do mirror writing. Unfortunately he is no longer available for engagement.

Even simple demonstrations can be inherently self-destructive. Nobody can reassemble the eggs to repeat the omelette. It is impossible to stick the stalks back on a bunch of roses cut for a flower arrangement. If there is time to do full rehearsals or there is the opportunity to run through everything for cameras in the studio then there must be a good supply of duplicate ingredients. Even the gung ho director who reckons never to need a full rehearsal or a second take can still be banjaxed if the floor manager drops the only box of eggs five minutes to air time.

Demonstrations can be messy

The director and floor manager have to agree whether it is quicker to do a bit of washing and cleaning in between rehearsals and the performance, or whether to have duplicates ready to set in at the last moment. Cleaning up the set may mean also cleaning up the demonstrator; oily or inky hands can give the game away. There should always be spare aprons at the ready. One food and drink programme has distinguished itself on occasions by coming to a demonstrator already splashed with wine stains who has to bluff herself through the implied message that she can't keep her hands off the booze before going on air or doesn't know how to use a corkscrew.

Many demonstrations involve part of the process which

has a built-in longueur. Baking a cake is the classic illustration. Everything flows beautifully until the oven door is shut and the oven temperature set. The viewer cannot be expected to wait an hour and a half to find out what the result looks like. On live shows the way out is to produce a finished item. The words 'And here's one I prepared earlier' has gone into the public consciousness as a catch phrase. Of course if some editing is available and the studio can be usefully employed in the meantime this time lag can simply be covered by a shot of a clock or a visual effect like a fade to black.

Blocking the shots and the stagger through

There is sometimes no possibility of a full rehearsal for the studio cameras. The time may only allow for a brief blocking in of the essential shots. This is also the time simultaneously for any last minute setting of microphones and tweaking of the lights. What can be achieved is to assign the required shots to the cameras and making sure that:

1   The shots are possible.
2   The cameras can get them without shooting each other or crowding in to each other.
3   There will be enough time to steady cameras and find focus. It is usually easier to reset the position of objects on the table than ask a camera to jump through hoops of fire.
4   The camera operators know the sequence of events and know which close-ups are which camera's responsibility.

If there is time the director give as full a briefing as possible and the demonstrator should be asked to go through the whole performance in dumb show, ideally twice, once continuously to give the camera crew an idea of the entire performance and a second time stopping and starting to allow the director to resolve any problems. If a third run as a complete dress rehearsal is possible so much the better. The director with this luxury still has to keep an eye on the performance. It is possible to over-rehearse and successive performances can decline in quality.

Directing tips

1 Most simple studio demonstrations can be successfully covered with two cameras. The demonstrators 'chat' camera stays at all times on the whole action and the other covers the close-ups. A third camera may be a luxury and can be used to cover particularly difficult close shots or cutaways of the demonstrator's face and reactions. A third camera will be needed if there is an anchor or other person reacting or making comments. There are also some demonstrations such as model making which demand a shot from high over the shoulder. A third camera will be needed to cover this – once in position the over-the-shoulder camera will be stuck for the duration and probably can only offer a single shot.

2 Directors should avoid the temptation to cut to a close-up every time the demonstrator makes a reference. If the line is 'and next take a pint of milk' it will be quite obvious in the wide shot what is going on and we all know what a pint of milk looks like.

3 Cut on action. Static cutaway shots can look as fake in a live studio demonstration as in an edited single camera one. If there is no natural action try to create some. If the flower arranger is going to introduce scissors, wire, ribbons or whatever make sure the components are at least pointed at. Remember that covering a demonstration is very close to drama directing.

4 Be very aware of focus. Bench-top demonstrations using small objects need skilled camerawork. The cameras will have to be physically very close to the work surface and even then will have to refocus on each object or action in turn. It is no good trying to pull the cameras back and shooting on the end of the zoom lens. As we have pointed out in describing the grammar of television the narrower the lens angle the shorter the depth of field. If it is difficult holding focus close up on a wide angle it will be impossible from further away. From the run-through the camera operators must know the sequence of

events and be able to anticipate them. The director will still have to work hard and will have to warn the close-up camera where to go and allow time for the shot to be steady and in focus.

'On you Two until he picks the glass up. One next. On One, Two the whisk next. Steady Two. Thanks Two. Pan with her to the bowl. Vinegar on Three next. Three. Tilt to the oil. Radishes on Two next. Wide shot on One.'

and so on. The cameras and particularly the vision mixer want to know the next shot or two ahead. Anticipation is the clue to a good studio demonstration. If things start to go wrong the temptation is for cameras to try to be helpful and improvise. Close-up cameras should hold their shots and resist following the action. A demonstration cannot be directed like a football match. Above all the main 'chat' camera should not zoom or tilt to lose any part of the action. The wide shot of the demonstration is the director's one fail-safe covering shot. To lose it is to dice with disaster.

7
Presenters

The relationship between the director and a presenter is always a delicate one. If there is a personality clash, or one doubts the abilities of the other the production is in danger of coming apart in recrimination. Some television personalities seem to thrive on creative tension; others will do almost anything for a quiet life. There is always the danger of a power struggle. Frequently presenters have achieved some fame and celebrity status. When the public come up to a unit in the street it is the presenter they recognize and greet, not the director. This can cause resentment. Presenters may get ideas above their station in life and demand to have their ways in both the production and direction of a programme. They may justify this as the result of working with untrained and inexperienced younger directors. Too often though it is a case of vanity and arrogance.

Conversely an old established director may be quite inattentive to the problems of an inexperienced younger presenter and forget that appearing on the screen is always a stressful experience. Just as a celebrity presenter gets all the public admiration, when things go wrong it is the presenter who is left exposed to public ridicule. Presenting can be a lonely and frightening experience. Good presenters, skilled both in the studio and on location, are few and rare. The star performers attract some of the highest fees in broadcasting. In consequence people with no special skill or training are propelled in front of camera by cost-cutting organizations. Since many of the great names of the past began their careers as journalists it has come to be thought that any journalist working in television can make a presenter. The horrid reality appears nightly.

A presenter is a performer as much as a reporter. Dressing up a young reporter with a trench coat and a stick microphone does not disguise a disagreeable manner, a repellent appearance, incoherent diction or a personality by-pass. It is becoming rarer for first time presenters to be put in the hands of an experienced director, or to have any direction at all. Without nurturing and guidance all the poor beginner can do is try to ape the mannerisms of others. This is all very unfair on everybody, particularly the viewers. For the professional beginner, or the expert brought in to present on camera, there are a number of tips. They apply to both studio and location working.

Preparation

1   What are you trying to tell the viewers and how much time have you to say it? One point made tellingly is better than a set of complex propositions which serve to bewilder the viewer. Clarity is all.

2   Check the facts and figures. Whether you do your own research or are given a brief go for the most telling points and keep clear of qualifications or generalizations.

3   Remember you are telling a story. Even the pettiest local news report must have a clear narrative line. If your contribution is of the intro and outro stereotype make sure that they relate to each other.

4   Look for ways to capture and hold the attention of the audience. A dramatic set of images may be a far better way to start than a shot of yourself staring at a camera. If you are beginning on camera try to think of an amusing or compelling opening shot. End the story with a telling turn of phrase or a memorable image. Never conclude by stating 'one thing is certain'. It almost never is anything of the sort.

5   Prepare some sort of crib for the main headings of your presentation. Where there is no autocue in a studio a set of postcards can be useful. Do not be embarrassed to use 'idiot boards', the main points written in large letters on a big sheet of cardboard held under the lens. If you are referring to exact facts and figures this may be essential. Unless you are very confident do not rehearse and learn your lines word for word, you risk losing any spontaneity and naturalness in delivery, as well as very likely fluffing the lines time and again. Some reporters

have devised the cunning idea of writing their lines, recording them on a sound cassette and then repeating them to camera whilst listening to a playback through a deaf-aid earpiece. A few top presenters can do this and still sound normal. Most cannot. The usual result is a completely false sounding delivery and the 'plonking' style.

6   Without attempting to be word perfect rehearse before a recording. If there is a director present ask for comments on the performance and delivery. Nobody is their own best judge and a member of the team might be able to suggest a turn of phrase or an impressive gesture. At worst they might point out the dandruff on your collar. A rehearsal is also useful for timing. Beginners invariably underestimate the time factor. The place to make cuts is before recording when there is a chance to rewrite and paraphrase. Last minute in the edit suite can render the story unintelligible.

Performance tips

1   You are the intermediary for the viewer; a mixture of guide, teacher and actor. Pitch your performance according to the subject matter. Do not present news about the local football team in tones appropriate for announcing the outbreak of war. Be relaxed in speech and manner and try to engage the audience's interest. Never hector the viewers.

2   Avoid like the plague the use of a 'plonking' style of delivery. In the early days of autocue news readers frequently had to read late stories off a screen line by line with no idea of how sentences were constructed or going to end. The result was a series of amusing but totally inappropriate stresses on words and syllables. 'Today in Zim BA bwe the Trade Minister said add RES sing the rally to MARK the anniversary of Inde PEN dence...'

Unlike Italian the English language does not have regular stresses, or a constant rhythm. English is a highly inflected language. Remember the children's game of permutating the stresses on words like 'A man eating rabbit...a MAN eating rabbit, a MAN-EATING rabbit, a man eating RABBIT, a man EATING rabbit' and so on. Speak with the appropriate stresses of ordinary conversation. Using the 'plonking' speech pattern does not add authority to the message. It suggests that you do not understand what you are saying.

3   Try to appear relaxed. If the presentation is from a desk sit upright but do not slouch. You are most likely to appear in mid-shot or mid close-up so avoid moving from side to side of the screen, or shifting from foot to foot. Slight movement towards the screen though can look a natural way to emphasize a point.

4   Look straight at the camera lens. You are talking one-to-one to a person at home and not addressing a crowd or making an official statement. Any loss of personal eye contact is disturbing and looks shifty. The only exception is when you may have to look away to consult facts and figures on a script or a monitor screen.

5   Think about how you use your hands. In a long shot or a mid-shot they can be expressive and if you use your hands naturally when talking then do so. If you are out with a single camera operator/recordist you may have no choice but to use a stick mike and hold a clip board. If you can free your hands by using a gun mike or personal microphone and throw away the board so much the better. Their main uses are as a comfort blanket. Do watch recordings of your performances to see if your hand movements appear natural and expressive or if they are only irritating mannerisms. Be very careful about florid hand movements if appearing at a desk; hands flailing in and out of close shots can be very annoying.

6   Use everyday conversational language. Those with a radio background are trained in the difference between writing for the spoken word and writing for print. Print journalists often are not. Use short sentences and simple words. Never forget that humour can be conveyed by inflection or facial expression and use both. There is not a lot of television which is

deadly serious despite what many practitioners like to tell themselves. You are a normal quirky human being, not a cloned journalistic automaton.

7   Since in almost all cases your performance will be cut in and out of a lengthier programme remember that a cut looks easier if motivated by a movement, however slight that may be. Studio presenters often employ the trick of giving a slight turn to or from an imaginary monitor screen at the beginning and end of their links. If a cut comes earlier or later than anticipated, then they are not found staring at the screen like rabbits facing a ferret. The same applies on location. If the direction demands a walking/talking shot it is best to step back a couple of paces and start walking before delivering the first words. Cutting to a static presenter who talks before the first step looks very silly. So can a forced and melodramatic turn aside.

Directing presenters

If the presenter is to appear at his or her best the director has obligations. Beginners may need all manner of help and reassurance. Professionals may be available for short periods only and if not directed properly can turn in a robotic performance. Amateurs may become overwhelmed and confused by the novelty of television production. Never take your eyes off the presenter when giving instructions or offering advice. This is particularly so when talking from the gallery to a presenter on the studio floor. The look on the face will tell immediately whether the direction has been understood or whether bewilderment has ensued. Studio is more intimidating than location shooting but on either it is easy for the director to get caught up in the mechanics of cameras and lights leaving the presenter unhappy and ignored. At any appropriate time the director should feel able to offer helpful advice and suggest improvements to a performance. Most presenters will appreciate this so long as the criticism is constructive. Even old established star performers need such input. The best known household names in the business easily drop into the trap of repeating their same repertoire of idiosyncrasies until they become parodies of themselves.

Preparation

1   Do not pile too much onto a presenter. If you are providing the research then provide it in a readily digested, comprehensible form. A two-minute introduction with a three-minute interview does not justify a whole dossier of information and press cuttings. A single sheet of A4 paper is quite adequate to contain all the main points, essential facts and proposed lines of questioning.

2   If the presenter is new give the fullest, earliest briefing about what is his anticipated role, the nature of the programme and target audience and how active a part is being suggested. It is one thing to roll up to a studio to record a simple set of links between videotape clips. It is another to carry a live programme which involves elements of interview, discussion or demonstration. Get this agreed and make sure contracts are signed before the recording day. The worst possible start will be a resentful presenter who feels put upon.

3   If any kind of script exists make sure it gets to the presenter as early as possible. Confirm in writing the details of studio times, location calls, transport arrangements and the like.

4   Be clear about how long you will need your presenter. On a location shoot it is likely that there will be no need for the presenter to rendezvous with the rest of the unit at the start of the day. Since many professionals have a number of commitments they will not appreciate being booked for hours before they are needed. Hanging about uselessly does nothing for a performance. It is notable how many professional presenters have become adept at crossword puzzles in consequence.

5   Always make sure that the presenter is met and welcomed. Always introduce him or her to the crew members on location and the floor manager and other key personnel in the studio.

6   If it is inevitable that studio camera rehearsals or other items cause delays do not keep presenters hanging around. Agree when they will be needed

and where they will be found and let them go to a canteen or a rest area.

7   If the presenter is having to link in and out of videotape inserts give them a chance to see these in advance. It will help them to prepare for the in and out cues and their reactions, a head turn, a smile or look of concern as appropriate.

8   During rehearsals there may have to be any number of interruptions or repeated takes for any number of technical reasons. It is too easy for the presenter to get paranoid and feel that is all his or her fault. Keep giving reassurance and encouragement through the floor manager or talkback and if there are major changes always explain why they have to be made.

9   During rehearsal and during long videotape inserts in a programme lower the studio lights. It is easier on the eyes.

10   If you are using autocue make sure that it is close enough to read with ease but not so close that the face appears distorted or the close-up shots reveal the eyes flickering as they scan the lines of text. Around 3 metres from the reader is probably the optimum distance. If a presenter is new to autocue make sure they can practise beforehand. Newcomers sometimes do not realize that the prompter follows their own speed of delivery, not that they have to keep up with the machine. The comic result can be the reader going faster and faster to keep up and the prompter accelerating to chase after him in turn. Reading from autocue is a difficult skill and at times the director may decide it better to dispense with it and return to a traditional script or idiot boards.

11   Make sure that the presenter knows what the floor manager's signals mean and on location is familiar with the language of direction. Unless the director is clear and precise it is very easy for a presenter to confuse rehearsals with real recordings and to miss or misunderstand cues. One advantage of the film clapperboard was that it indicated unequivocally when a real take was going on.

12   Decide whether the presenter wants or can benefit

from talkback. Presenters receive talkback through a deaf aid earpiece. Professionals carry their own. Newcomers may have to be fitted. Ideally there should be one for each ear so that there is a choice depending on the setting and lighting. In an interview set-up the furthest, upstage ear is less noticeable. There are two types of talkback: omnibus talkback includes all the sounds and dialogue coming from the control gallery and other technical areas; switch talkback enables the director to talk directly to a presenter at the press of a switch. With neither can the presenter reply directly unless an open microphone is at hand. Omnibus talkback is for the professional presenter who can interpret the chaos of voices and signals to understand everything that is going on. It can reduce any beginner to a nervous wreck. Switch talkback is an essential minimum for the director to tell a presenter about script changes, timings and cues on a live programme. The presenter will need a familiarity with the technology before using it. In times of crisis the use of talkback can be disguised by a dummy telephone on a presenter's desk. It makes it easier for the audience to accept the fiction of a dialogue between director and presenter. Total beginners are better off relying on the floor manager alone. It is the job of the floor manager to strike up an easy relationship with the presenter.

13   Check the physical appearance of the presenter. There should always be available brushes, combs and simple make-up. Lights may bring on shiny faces and gleaming bald patches. Hair may become dishevelled, collars crooked, hems not straight. Presenters may be sensitive about comments on their appearance and choice of clothes but it is the job of the director to point out weaknesses and suggest remedial action.

8
On location

Shooting on location presents infinite possibilities for catastrophe ranging from manslaughter through to copyright, contracts, defamation, trespass, insurance, confidentiality, bribery and the specific problems of working with children and animals. A fuller description of these horrors is to be found in the sister volume of this book *The Essential Television Handbook*.

No two directors will approach location shooting in the same way. Everyone has eventually to work out an individual style and method. A lot depends on the genre of the programme.

Figure 8.1

If we just consider factual or documentary programme styles there are presenter-led stories, programmes with out-of-vision commentary alone, fly-on-the-wall observational series, dramatized documentaries, archive-based historical subjects, investigative current affairs reports, travelogues and all sorts of combinations of these. Whether the item is a four-minute motoring magazine slot or a documentary series on the treasures of the Vatican Library there are a series of stages through which the director ought to progress.

Research

It may seem obvious to state but the director ought always to know what he or she is trying to achieve and why the camera is going on a particular location, yet this is very often overlooked or skimped. The director is first and foremost a storyteller. An interesting subject is not a story. An attractive location is not a subject. Discovering the narrative line and finding the locations and performers to tell the story about the subject is what research is about and the main thing that directors and producers are paid for. In a sense everything else about the job is technique. So if the subject is the British Love of Animals it is not enough to say 'let's go to a donkey sanctuary and see if we can get an interview and some nice pictures'. What particular aspect of the story is the shoot going to cover? Is it how the owners battled to raise money? Is it to hear tales of neglect and cruelty? Has the charity been misappropriating the funds? Why has this location been chosen over others and what is likely to look good on camera when you get there? Under no circumstances should a director take the journalist's idle way out by writing a commentary in advance and then going on location to try and pick up some appropriate pictures to cover the words. Such shots are contemptuously known as 'wallpaper' in the business.

Research can involve many things and a skilled researcher is a vital member of any production team which can afford one. Where the subject matter is very specialized it is usual to contract an academic or professional consultant to provide and supervise research material. If the director has to conduct his or her own research the first task is to locate the sources of material whether in reference books, press cuttings and picture libraries, or recently, electronic sources like the World Wide Web. The most valuable source is conversation. Talk to as many people as possible and do so wherever possible face to face. The telephone is only a second best. Fax and e-mail are last resorts. If this involves late evening trips to people's houses or a certain amount of liquid lubrication so be it; only face to face do people divulge anecdotes and rumours and utter gross indiscretions which can give the director invaluable storylines and leads. Meeting face to face is vital if there is a suggestion of using someone on camera. Talking to chance acquaintances can be as fruitful as talking to a main informant. The consultant heart surgeon at a hospital may be a main contributor but the hospital receptionist may be able to dish the dirt about salmonella in the canteen as well as give practical advice about good times to shoot, interesting coming events, and the best pub in the neighbourhood. Electronic communications have opened up unparalleled access to research material but in other ways they have become a curse. E-mail is fine for communicating factual material but an e-mail conveys none of the dimensions of a proper human conversation. It tells you nothing about the sincerity or articulateness of the correspondent or whether he or she has a stutter and unintelligible accent, is placid or prickly, or for that matter is on the verge of a nervous breakdown and a hopeless alcoholic.

The recce

The reconnaissance or recce is the essential prelude to any location shoot. (A recce is a British military term regarded as pompous where American English is spoken. Americans describe the activity as 'a scouting' which gives rise to reciprocal hilarity amongst the British.) Depending on the urgency of the story, and the time and distance involved, a location recce can take anything from 20 minutes to a full day. With an outside broadcast there may be more than a single recce needed, one for editorial purposes and a second for a technical site visit. The worst possible start to a shoot is for the director to arrive at a rendezvous with the crew and ask 'how do you see it?' They will be entitled to retreat to their cars and refuse to budge until the director has made up his mind. An alternative response will be to treat the director with deserved contempt and delegate to him the organizing of mugs of tea whilst they wander off to look for any likely shots. The result at least will be a phenomenal shooting ratio of largely unwanted shots which do not cut together. Even if a prior visit is impossible the director should make a point of getting to the location early and making a tour of the site and confirming the availability of interviewees. If the team travels together the director and camera operator should conduct a joint tour to plan the shooting day before unpacking a single piece of equipment. Without this precaution the crew will be doomed to cross and recross their tracks randomly either duplicating shots or missing important ones. It is a necessary piece of courtesy to introduce the crew to interviewees, location owners and anyone else whose cooperation is wanted.

It is impossible to list all the problems to look for on a recce. The great pleasure of location filming is that no two locations ever turn up the same challenges. Directing is a business of constant learning from experience, generally through mistakes. With experience the director develops a sixth sense about locations. Lurking problem areas can be sniffed out as soon as the intended location is approached. For the beginner the following checklist should help.

Lighting
1 Are lights necessary?
Modern video cameras and lenses have great light sensitivity and with their electronic 'gain' can get acceptable exposures in most conditions. But lighting is not just about illumination. Simple portrait lighting can lift the quality of even a simple interview. If any particular mood is to be established in an interior setting additional lights will be essential. If the programme is a drama, or there is a large interior to be covered, the camera operator ought to be with the director on the recce. The crew may need to bring an extra sparks (lighting electrician). The 'headlight' camera strapped to the top of news cameras is an abomination, technically next to useless and producing hideously ugly results. Lights take extra time to rig but are well worth the trouble. It may be technically clever and cheap to film down a drain without any lights but if the images are flat and ugly the programme will suffer. Some documentary directors may quite rightly choose to sacrifice picture quality for the unobtrusiveness or

flexibility which comes with no extra lighting. The choice must be deliberate, not the result of oversight. The crew needs to know in advance what sort of lighting rig is required. It is no good finding out on location that the equipment is inappropriate or the crew left the lamps back at base.

2 What is the position of the sun?

If it is decided to leave lighting to the Great Sparks In The Sky the position of the sun for the time of year may be critical. In winter shooting hours may be very limited. If weather is poor the shooting day will have to be planned around the opportunities for filming exteriors. On sunny winter days the sun is low in the sky and may shine directly into the camera lens. What can be shot in the morning with the sun in the east may be impossible in the afternoon when it is in the west. This can be important for some interiors. A church with stained glass windows can change constantly during the day. This can play havoc with continuity. If the architecture is important the shoot must be planned around the times when the windows and the aisles are seen at their best. At least the orientation of a church is always the same. For other exteriors the director might take a compass and map and check sunrise and sunset times in the newspapers.

3 What technical limitations are there?

Where are the available power sockets and what is their amperage? Is there any odd voltage like the 110 volt systems used in some industrial premises? How far from the scene is the main fusebox and should the crew bring an extra cable run to get to the power supply? Old buildings, village halls and the like often have small and rickety wiring systems and the expedient of stuffing a hairpin in a fuse box to take the extra location lights can result at best in sudden blackout or at worst a conflagration; only a professional electrician should start messing about with plugs or wiring on location. Lights should all be fitted with safety glasses and chains if suspended. One of the worrying aspects of multiskilling and short crewing is that people are being expected to do things away from their specialist skills and this can put people and property at risk. Even a simple house may pose problems. There may be apparently plenty of sockets but which are power points and which are domestic lighting circuits?

4 Are there administrative problems?

Does the location owner require his own local electrician to be present and will this entail overtime payments or an agreed gratuity? Are there any fire insurance problems with the location? If existing theatrical lighting is to be used has the relevant Trade Union branch been informed? Will you be expected to pay for the power used? Are there areas where ordinary film lights are banned? Some places such as flour mills or coal mines may even ban electrically operated equipment. Lights are probably the most hazardous things on a location shoot. Lighting stands are generally flimsy and not very stable. Lamps become dangerously hot. Cables stretched across pavements or corridors are accidents waiting to happen. Lamp bulbs can explode with literally blinding results. Many commercial premises will forbid the laying of cables across stairs and landings or along corridors and forbid the blocking open of fire doors. You may need hazard tape. Always check with the resident Health and Safety officer.

Sound

Pity the poor recordist, always doomed by the priority of pictures to playing second fiddle to the camera. Sound has always been the element most likely to be forgotten by the director, yet even in news programmes the quality of the sound, or its absence, can make or break a story. This seems to be a source of repeated astonishment to management executives. There seems to be an impression that sensible microphones and even recordists themselves are redundant. Two more abominations which have crossed over from home video to broadcasting are built-in camera microphone and the automatic sound gain control. No professional should rely on either. The automatic control measures all ambient sound and theoretically maintains a steady recording level. It does not measure intelligibility. It might suffice to record one person speaking directly to camera in a silent room. But locations are not silent. The moment a lorry passes by, the automatic control hears the increased volume of noise and lowers the recording level. The voice level drops to a whisper drowned by engine noise. The lorry passes, the background is quiet and the voice suddenly soars operatically. A distant factory stops work and the presenter starts to shout. A speaker with a sea shore or motorway for a background will go unheard as the machine compensates for the roar of traffic or the thunder of waves on shingle. Cheap and nasty sound recording is the mark of cheap and nasty programming. The sound problems ought to be thought out at the recce.

1 Which sorts of microphones are needed?

The favourite all-purpose microphone is the directional or rifle mike. A recordist is essential to hold it. If the recordist is to effectively monitor sound or attempt to mix more than one track on location there may need to be someone else to hold the microphone, particularly if its to be mounted on a hand-held boom. For some interview situations a pair of personal clip-on microphones may be the choice. Most modern cameras have two soundtracks so a compromise solution is to record two soundtracks simultaneously and sort out a balance in post production. For distant or moving shots there is a need for radio microphones. For walking interviews or distant dialogue at least two will be needed. The most useless and alas most commonly seen location microphone is the hand-held stick mike. This will give better quality than an abysmal camera mounted microphone but otherwise should be regarded as a wand of office for reporters who do not know what else to do with their hands.

2 What are the local sound problems?

Directors can become so caught up with their story that they become oblivious to the most appalling racket during a recce. Is there an obvious source of disturbance like a school playground next door or an airport flight path overhead? When is the local rush hour? In a rural scene is there an electric milking parlour nearby? Is there any forestry work where chain saws are used? A recording can be ruined by a chain saw working a couple of miles away. Sod's Law dictates that on the day of the recce the schools are on holiday, the foresters are planting saplings and there is an air traffic controllers' strike. On the day of the shoot all hell breaks loose. Even if the problems may be unavoidable the director can minimize them by planning the shooting day. School playtimes and rush hours are at predictable times. Choosing to shoot interviews on a far side of a building may minimize background road noise. Flight paths can change. The

London Heathrow paths depend on wind direction. Most of West London is intolerable with planes passing low at less than two-minute intervals, but at some times the flight paths are switched and passable sound recordings are possible. It pays to ask local residents about noise. The information will not be volunteered if you don't ask.

3   Are there problems with ambient sound?

Industrial and commercial properties often have the curse of piped music in the background. It is vital to find how this can be switched off, at least temporarily during recording. Schools have bells, shops have public address systems, everywhere seems to sprout maintenance men with ghetto blaster radios. Can prior arrangements be made to have these turned off on the filming day? If not how can the locations be switched around to minimize the nuisance? Is it possible to change the day to a weekend which may be quiet? As a final check the director ought to stand absolutely still to listen to the atmosphere. The microphone will pick up loud and clear what the ear usually disregards. Two sounds that drive recordists insane are noisy air conditioning and ancient fluorescent lighting buzz.

Crew welfare

The least popular type of director is the one who is treated like a king by a managing director or landlord on the recce but fails to remember the problems of the technical crew. A director might well be taken to lunch in the boardroom, allowed to park in the chairman's space and given the key to the executive lavatory. The crew may have to fend for themselves unless arrangements are made. Tending to crew comforts is the best way to maintain enthusiasm for a shoot. Camera crews have to work day in, day out for a variety of different directors on all sorts of stories. They cannot be expected to share each director's passion for every new programme and they definitely will not if they feel neglected, overworked or exploited.

1   Getting there

Unless the entire unit is travelling in one vehicle it is important to tell everyone concerned clearly where to go and how and when to get there. There should be a written schedule with

A to Z photocopied street plans or ordinance survey maps with the best routes described. There should be contact telephone numbers in case of breakdown or delay. Times for the start and finish of the shooting should be indicated with main mealtimes. The schedule should take account of travelling times and time to pack up equipment. Crews will be unimpressed with the director who works them to the point of mutiny and then clears off for a drink leaving them to clear up and drive for several hours to the next location.

> **Word of warning**
> However well members of the production team know each other and however tedious the procedure, always make sure that everybody involved has a schedule with all the details including everybody's telephone, mobile and fax numbers with similar details about the location and interviewees. Never rely upon someone to pass the message on. If there are any changes do a completely new schedule and redistribute to all concerned. If there are repeated revisions copy on to different colour paper each time to avoid mistakes. One BBC production manager did once skimp the procedure when there was a late change of locations. The cast arrived at Kingston on Thames and the crew was sent to Kingston on Hull 200 miles away.

2 Access

Parking is always a vexed question. Are there enough spaces reserved for the number of vehicles? Are the spaces near to the main entrance? If on-street parking is needed have arrangements been made to suspend parking meters or obtain police permission? Is there a problem with local security guards and have individually named passes been issued? Are there strict times for opening and locking premises and who holds the keys? Where is it best to offload the equipment, and where are the best lifts? Remember that goods and service lifts and back entrances are often the most convenient. It has been observed that most of filming time seems to be occupied by lifting boxes in and out of cars, one could add in and out of lifts and up and down stairs. Short crewing has meant that there are no longer spare pairs of hands on a crew. Even the new handicam scale cameras do not completely solve the problems. If lack of planning means that the equipment has to be dropped and the crew vehicle then driven off to look for a parking space, that same driver is likely to be the camera operator or the recordist. Every hour spent driving around is a very expensive hour off the filming time. In places like central London the crew vehicle can vanish for an eternity.

3 Personal welfare

Does the location demand special clothing? Don't imply that the shooting will be in a centrally heated office and then announce that there are a few shots needed in a pig farm or on a fishing boat. Are there male and female lavatories on site? When and where is the catering provided? It may be unavoidable to have to eat in the works canteen but the crew should be warned and not dragooned if they would prefer to sit in the van eating sandwiches. Can coffee or tea be provided at the start of the day? A thoughtful director will carry an industrial-sized thermos flask and buy a packet or two of biscuits. An inconsiderate one will meet the crew and demand to start shooting immediately. A smart one will have recced pubs in the vicinity, made arrangements for breaks to fit in with kitchen times and pay for the first round of lunchtime drinks.

4 Safety

Many locations demand protective clothing, hard hats, protective headgear and so on. These items may have to be arranged locally or brought to the location. But if there are any plans to shoot from scaffolding, up chimneys, on the water or on motorways the crew must be forewarned about the safety implications. Safety lines for operators and equipment may be required, fluorescent jackets for filming near a highway or life jackets for filming on water may have to be ordered, only the recce will pinpoint the problems.

Directing the camera

Watch any television drama shot on film on location. Before each take the same ritual is performed.

| Director (or first assistant) | 'Quiet please! Going for a take! Standby!' |
| Camera operator | 'Board in please' (assistant puts clapper board in shot). |

Director	'Turn over'.
Camera operator	'Running'.
Recordist	'Sound running!' or 'speed!'
Camera operator	'Mark it'.
Camera assistant	'Scene thirty-four take three' (claps the board).
Director	'Action!' or 'Cue!'

And at the conclusion of each take always the magic word:

Director	'CUT!'

There are permutations of the ritual familiar to anyone brought up on shooting with film. Some takes will not need sound. In this case the ritual is performed as above but with a mute board, e.g. the board is presented already closed. If the camera operator has to react fast to an action the ritual is reserved until the finish of the tape.

Director	'End-board!'
Camera operator	'Mark it!'
Assistant	(puts board in front of lens, upside down). 'Thirty-four take four!' (claps board).
Director	'Cut!' (only then do both sound and camera stop recording).

The word Action is self-explanatory. The alternative word Cue is reserved for artists' lines or technical changes, e.g. Cue the lighting change! Cue the extras! Cue him! or Cue her!

This little performance, familiar now at second hand to most viewers from a hundred feature films, has a number of functions. Technically film is a little more complex than videotape. Sound and pictures are recorded separately and remain apart until the final stage of post production. The clapper board is essential to identify each shot in vision and to give a sound cue for the picture editor to put sound and pictures into synchronism. As video usually has synchronous sound and identifies shots by built-in time code this part of the procedure may be redundant. Plenty of directors though still resort to a marked-up board at the beginning of scenes even if the clap itself is no longer needed. When looking through miles of rushes and scenes out of sequence it can be quicker to pick out scene numbers than watch and note endless telephone numbers flashing across the screen. The main purposes of the ritual remain important regardless of the technology.

1   From the first call of 'Quiet please!' 'Standby everybody!' the entire crew and cast are aware that the take is for real. This includes anyone else within ear shot whether make-up artists, drivers, runners or rubber necking members of the public.

2   The call 'Turn over!' instructs the technical crew to go into action. Their replies assure the director that all is OK. If the sound recordist has not run up to operating speed, or the board is not in focus or the camera is not steady they will say so. It is also a last chance for performers to announce they may not be ready.

3   The call 'Action!' is given only when the director is assured that artists and crew are all prepared.

4   The call 'Cut!' tells the whole unit they can relax whilst the camera crew check the take by running back some of the recorded tape, or checking the film gate in the camera for any debris (hairs). The ultimate message is 'A clear!' from the camera operator to inform the director that the take is technically satisfactory. The entire ritual ensures crystal clear communication between the director, the crew, the performers and ultimately the film editor.

The arrival of videotape as the main recording medium coincided with the shrinking of crew sizes. Both happened at the same time as the recruitment of large numbers of entrants who had never known film or often had a journalistic background with only the fuzziest idea about cameras. The result was a wholesale abandonment of the language of direction. Out went the bath water and out went the babies.

Contrast the above with a contemporary scene.

Journalist   (turns from interviewee to camera operator) 'Did you get all that?'

Operator   'Sorry?'

Journalist   'That bit about the war, did you get it?'

Operator	'Sorry I didn't think we were recording yet.'
Journalist	'What about the earlier wartime stuff.'
Recordist	'The bit where those goods trains went past?
Operator	'It will be there somewhere, we're on roll five already.'
Journalist	'Do you think we've got enough yet?'
Operator	'I'll bash off a couple of rolls of exteriors if you like.'
Journalist	'I thought you'd done that.'
Operator	'No, but I kept running when we were in the car. I thought you might need some shots.'

In many stations things have come to the pass where camera operators have never encountered proper camera direction and object when they do. It is likely that those who resent direction most are those most in need of it. A small crew, a small budget and a desperate deadline will militate against the location discipline. But always the director, and that also includes any journalist in charge, has to establish some routine.

The director must know the beginnings and ends of shots. This means that there must always as a very minimum be the instruction 'Turn over!' and the camera operator and recordist must signal that they are prepared to go on.

'Action' is essential for anything from a close-up of a hand picking up a beer glass to ten soldiers leaping out of a trench. It is a universally known command even used in countries where not another word of English is understood. It does not have to be bellowed at the top of the voice so long as it is clear. Curiously some directors appear too bashful to bring themselves to utter the word.

'Cut' is vital. It is not for the camera operator to decide when a shot is finished. The director must know what is going on the tape. It has got to be established that the operator will wait for instructions and the director will be relied upon to give them.

The good news
Videotape cassettes run several times longer than a roll of film and at a fraction of the cost. This means that a director need not be so punctilious about stopping and starting between successive shots. If a director does not want to cut there should be the instruction 'Keep running' until the desired

cut point is reached. This can be very valuable where an interview goes to pieces but the director decides it best to repeat questions and keep going without stopping for a retake.

The bad news

Incompetent directors reckon that by keeping the camera running and eating up miles of tape they will eventually arrive at what they want. The analogy of a thousand monkeys at a thousand typewriters trying to write *Hamlet* does spring to mind.

> **Helpful hint**
> Having got into the discipline of calling 'Turn over!', 'Action!' and 'Cut!' do not get carried away. The absent member of the team is the picture editor. Depending on the model of equipment, video recorders take anything up to six seconds to get to a stable running speed. So the director should not shout 'Turn-over-action!' without giving the video camera operator and recordist time. The operator should call 'Speed!' when ready. The 'Action' call must be delayed. An interviewer or reporter should not rush to speak immediately on the word Cue. There should be ample time to draw breath. A count of two or three seconds before starting a speech or movement is very helpful to the editor. The commonest fault is to bellow 'Cut!' immediately on the last word of a take. A picture editor needs a brief pause to locate the best cutting point for sound as well as picture.
>
> A dramatic end to an interview may be a silent second or so on the face of a guest. The best cutting point for someone passing through frame might be on a turn, or leaving the edge of frame. A director's voice on the sound track can create terrible sound editing problems. If the director's voice overlaps speech or an important sound effect the editor is completely compromised.

No two locations are the same and no two directors will operate in exactly the same way or have the same style. The common factor is that he or she must shoot with editing in mind. And however well resourced a programme seems to be there is never, never enough time available for editing. The mark of the good director is an ability to use the shooting time to the best advantage and to minimize the problems in post production. Necessity is the mother of invention and the director has often to fall back on imagination and improvisation. The following are some well-tried tips.

1 Never forget that the viewer only sees what you want him to see. Do not rush about from spot to spot trying to ring the changes. For example, if the camera is suitably placed in a street or market there are at least four distinct backgrounds available as the camera pans around 360°. Whether the intention is a set of short interviews or just a montage of interesting shots it is better to look for one good camera position and exploit all its possibilities rather than leap about taking a shot here and a shot there.

2 You are usually shooting out of the editing sequence. Plan to do the different set-ups in a logical sequence for the location. Minimize the number of physical moves between set-ups to maximize the shooting time at each one.

3 Do not deceive yourself about what can be achieved. There are only so many set-ups that can be achieved in a day even with good planning. About six minutes cut footage per shooting day is a reasonable target to aim for with a documentary programme and half that for anything involving dramatization. Talk it through with the camera operator at the start of the day. If it looks like the schedule is wildly over-optimistic decide which are vital shots, which are important, and which are optional. A decent camera operator will appreciate being taken into confidence and will offer all manner of solutions for completing the story in the time available. It is more likely that the crew will cooperate and agree an over-run if they are aware what the problems are. The worst sin a director can commit is to lie to the crew about the work involved.

4 Never think in terms of individual shots. Think in terms of dramatic sequences. The 'every-frame-a-Rembrandt' school of cinematography is only appropriate to unhurried and sumptuously financed

productions. The floors of the world's cutting rooms are paved with exquisite shots that did not add anything to the narrative or did not cut with any other shots. As the poet W. H. Auden advised young writers, 'Learn to murder your babies.'

5   Be economical. There is a Rule of Threes operating in television. Cameramen used to have as a mantra 'Wide shot, mid-shot, tight shot, wide shot, mid-shot, tight shot' and so on.

In almost any scene a wide establishing shot, a mid-shot showing the performer, and a series of tight shots of faces and actions will ensure that the picture editor has a minimal selection of shots which will edit together. Often all three can be obtained from a single camera position. For example, if the scene is a man cycling over a bridge the camera can begin with a wide angle of the bridge and cyclist in the distance, zoom in for a mid-shot of the performer approaching, and then either go for a very narrow-angle close-up or wait until the cyclist is closer and capture shots of pedals, handlebars, facial expression or whatever. They should all cut together. Single cutaways often stick out for what they are; acts of desperation. Three shots that cut together for the same purpose sometimes look like a creative decision.

6   Remember that the majority of pans or zooms are not necessary and do not work. When setting them up keep all the editing options open. Follow the Rule of Threes. In a simple sequence like panning from a road scene to a tower first compose the opening road scene and record for a minimum of ten seconds, perform the zoom to the tower, hold the end shot for ten seconds then zoom out back to the road and hold the shot. If the timing of the zoom may be critical repeat the whole procedure at a faster or slower speed. The editor now has every possible combination. The final decision in most cases will be to throw out all the movements and cut directly between the best street shot and the best static picture of the tower.

7   Never rush. Hold every shot for six to ten seconds as a minimum. This can feel a very long time when you are in a hurry. Both directors and camera operators under pressure often think that they have recorded six seconds when they have shot only three. If there is any focus problem or camera wobble or there is the sound of the director speaking six seconds may even be too short to be usable. A terrible sin is to let the camera continuously pan zoom without pause so that the editor is reduced to the crashingly obvious device of freeze frames to create shots that will cut.

8   If you are in a real hurry, have nobody to write a shot list and do not use a clapperboard you can still communicate with the absent picture editor. A presenter repeating shots to camera can indicate the number of each take by holding up the appropriate number of fingers before the beginning of each take. A cameraman, attempting a difficult move should 'flag' unsuccessful ones by waving an open hand across the lens after each bad take.

9   Think about sound. Far more problems arise in videotape editing from manipulating sound than from cutting the pictures. If music is involved, either as part of the action or an unavoidable background noise, always shoot a long continuous shot or series of shots without cutting the camera. Film has the advantage that sound may run continuously whilst the camera can film discontinuously. In video they are shackled together. Every location, even a quiet room, has a distinct acoustic. At the end of each set-up ask the recordist for an atmosphere or 'buzz' track. This is a couple of minutes when everyone is completely silent and a track of the ambient sound is recorded. If there have been interruptions like passing aeroplanes or heavy vehicles you should try to record some of these from distant approach to final departing echo. The editor can use these to smooth over awkward acoustic changes. The eye will accept all manner of picture cuts but the ear will reject any where there is uncomfortably discontinuous background sound.

10   Shots are always improved by movement. A simple shot of the exterior of an office is improved by figures walking past or through the doors. The figure concerned sometimes has to be a member of the team. Editing is always made easier with cuts motivated by action. A boring shot of a building can be given life by panning with a bus passing through shot and leaving frame. A track can be motivated by following a figure. Shots of a library an enlivened by close-ups of hands taking down volumes or searching catalogues. Keep note of continuity and always overlap both sound and movements in successive shots.

A word of warning
If shooting random members of the public as a way to add movement to a shot be very careful about the context. If possible warn them before or after the take. People can be defamed by pictures. One famous case was a programme about police corruption which was illustrated by an exterior shot of a police station and anonymous passers-by. Unfortunately the passers-by were plain clothes CID officers. Policemen are notoriously litigious and they claimed that they were recognizable to colleagues and thus in the context were being accused of corruption. The television company had to pay up.

9
Writing commentary

One of the most intractable problems that documentary directors face is how to persuade outsiders that the starting point for programmes is *not* a polished commentary script. To anyone with a theatrical background this would seem odd. Most television dramas start from a written screenplay even when the director comes to this through long periods of improvisation in rehearsal. Many journalists regard film and video the same as photographs in a newspaper, arresting and illustrative perhaps, but always subordinate to the writing.

Corporate clients and sponsors feel that they have a right to confirm every word of text before shelling out their money; managers flex their muscles by demanding to see typescripts. Not a few current affairs programmes have been made with an eye to publishing the commentary as a magazine article

Figure 9.1

subsequently. They are all wrong. Sadly this illusion has spread far and wide throughout contemporary television. There has always been the exception of news bulletins. Stories have to be written and rewritten up to the moment of transmission often more in hope than certainly that any pictures will have arrived and been edited in time. Picture editors regularly have to cut pictures in the absence of the journalist or producer responsible for the text. One journalist may be beavering at researching and writing a story whilst another is running around on location. Increasingly camera operators go out solo to collect appropriate visual material with not much idea of the thrust of the narrative. In this hectic world there has arisen a new priority. Write up the story first. Fit pictures to it where you can.

Since the 1980s journalists have spread into senior positions throughout every area of factual programming. With them has come the illusion that the written script takes automatic priority. Working methods that emerged of necessity for one-minute bulletin reports are assumed to be appropriate for hour long documentary features. This is a delusion. A lot which is dreary or confusing or cliché ridden in current television comes down to this effort to force pictures into a straitjacket of text. Television programmes are a composite of words and sounds and pictures. If the elements clash the pictures win every time. A picture has an immediate impact and instantly tells its own story. Commentary requires attention and takes time to sink in. Words at best complement the pictures; pictures cannot be made slaves to the words. A screenplay is a very different thing to a commentary script.

Many documentary makers rebel against the tyranny of the journalistic style and try to make programmes without any commentary whatsoever. If television really is primarily a visual medium this ought to be possible. A lot of very successful observational or 'fly-on-the-wall' programmes have been created with no narration or only the occasional line of commentary. The price to pay is often a huge shooting ratio and a long period in a cutting room working on the construction. Not all subjects are appropriate. Not every picture sequence is visually self-apparent. The necessary footage may be inadequate or inaccessible. There may have to be a written commentary. Writing commentary for television pictures is very different to writing a script for radio and even more unlike writing for a newspaper. Writing television commentary is a special skill. Fortunately it is a skill which any fully literate person can acquire.

Preparation

Leaving the commentary script to last does emphatically not mean going into production without knowing what the programme is setting out to say. Documentaries evolve throughout the production and post production processes. Commentary is part of the same evolution. Even fly-on-the-wall programmes dependent on unfolding events and no preconceived ending must start with a well-researched subject or a strong notional storyline. There is an implicit screenplay from the start; one of the delights of documentary making is watching how a story develops. Being ready to think on the feet, revise ideas and react to the unexpected are vital skills for a documentary director. Hobble the programme from the outset with a pre-existing written script and the production is doomed to plod along a predestined track.

Most productions start with a written brief. There is not much chance of raising a budget without submitting an outline treatment which proposes shooting days, locations, main contributors, archive material sources and so on. This will come after a research period and maybe after the preliminary recce.

When producers were salaried employees it was assumed that a great deal of their time would be spent chasing, developing and writing up programme proposals. It is far harder for today's freelance to persuade a broadcast company to finance this crucial development period. The completed outline will still be dependent on a complex budgeting procedure. So even before the show is allowed on the road there are rigid constraints and definite proposals. These might be summarized on one sheet of paper, or may be several thousand words long. What should not be submitted is the final commentary script. In one way, however, the commentary will already be appearing. Research will throw up quotations, illuminating facts and figures, anecdotes, documents, biographical details and newspaper stories. A recce will suggest interesting characters, suitable music, buildings, landscapes, monuments, street names, interiors, photo collections and no end of other possibilities. From the moment of their involvement the producer, director and researcher must constantly exchange ideas. The constant process of kicking ideas around an office or bouncing thoughts off other colleagues in the bar has been one casualty of fragmentation in the industry.

Playing in a one-man-band can be a lonely occupation. Cottage industries can get very introverted. Today original ideas are jealously guarded as 'intellectual capital' in a market dominated by short-term contracts and cut throat competition. But talk and more talk is the best way for ideas and phrases to surface, sink again or re-emerge in a final commentary script. Producers and directors who write commentaries need to be intellectual scavengers.

It pays to keep a notebook from the start. The success of the filming will progressively reveal how much written commentary is going to be needed, how far the picture sequences and interviews will be able to stand alone. A pocket cassette recorder can be invaluable and so, as an aide-mémoire, can be a Polaroid camera.

Editing

Post production procedures vary enormously. Some picture editors are highly dextrous technicians but want the director at their sides almost all the time to make all creative and editorial decisions. Some directors likewise want to be in complete control of every cut. Conversely many editors, particularly those whose training has been with film, prefer to work to a brief and without interference and make their own creative input. Plenty of directors have no affection for spending days in a video editing suite and would rather trust the editor for much of the time.

Ideally there should be a creative partnership. Nobody is best judge of their own work and an editor who comes fresh to the rushes will quickly pick up on shots and sequences that are not successful. Directors trying to do their own picture editing can suffer the equivalent of writer's block. The director is the ultimate decision maker but listening to the advice of the editor and trying out new ideas in the edit suite can transform a documentary. As one gastronomically inclined picture editor put it 'shooting is like going to the market but editing is like cooking the dish'. In which case the director is in charge of the menu.

With film editing it is common practice for the director and editor to sit together at an editing table to watch the rushes. The same applies with video if time allows. With many productions the best procedure is to have all the rushes initially transferred to VHS cassettes with time code in vision. The director can then go away and work at leisure, first on a shot list and second on an outline assembly order.

The shot list

The days are largely gone when every location shoot was accompanied by a PA to take notes and type out a nightly shot list. It is usually now a job left until the end of a shoot and increasingly the personal chore of the director. This need be no bad thing. A shot list may be as detailed or generalized as the director and editor will be happy with. A traditional detailed shot list might go:

Cassette 14	The Library Affair
Time	Shot
1.06	Presenter walks to table, lifts knife. n.g.
1.13	Take 2 as before, slowly. n.g.
1.20	Take 3 as before. ok.
2.35	Close-ups hand, different speeds
3.02	Pres. MCU turns to cam. Shows knife at
1.12	
5.25	MLS woman in chair

and so on

Alternatively a looser version might read:

Cassette 14	The Library Affair
Time	Shot
1.00–5.45	Pres. with murder weapon intro
4.12–10.00	Interview policeman. Take 2 best
10.00–12.15	Interview cutaways
15.50–end	G. V s library interiors

Generally the longer the story and the more complex the shooting the more detailed the shot list ought to be. There are few things more time wasting than an editor and director spooling back and forth through piles of cassettes looking for one lost cutaway or missing essential close-up.

The assembly script

Before the picture editor can begin to contribute she or he will need to know what the director wishes to communicate in each sequence and what is the intended dramatic structure of the programme. If the editor is a purely technical operator and the director totally in control the explanations can come during a joint viewing of the rushes. If the partnership is more equal the picture editor needs some kind of script. All documentaries are shot out of sequence and some directors may choose to edit scenes each at a time to be reassembled in a final order only later. Either way the assembly script is the first point where words and pictures start coming together on a paper.

The Library Affair

Sequence	Commentary	Music and effects
Titles. Montage B & W photos press headlines. Roll 9. Shots at 2.08– 15.00 also Roll 11 Shots between 7.00–11.30.		'Devil Rides Out' RPM CD 01998
Pres in vision. Synch Roll 14. shots 1.06–3.45.	'Nobody thought that... ...her cut throat.'	
Manor exteriors. Roll 4 shots 14.20 to end. Also Roll 2 1230–1500 Pres. out of vision.	Describes history of family inheritance.	Thunder(?) Wind effects.
Library interiors	Describes scene of murder. Footsteps, creaking door.	
Pres. out of vision Library interiors Roll 14 13.50 to end, Roll 15 1.15–10.35.	Bloodstains. Missing Bible.	
Interview vicar Roll 2 Question Village reactions 3.00–4.00, possibly retake 16.40–	ends...'even today people will not talk about it'.	

17.10 Cutaways
beginning roll 3.

News Footage BBC/	Describes public interest.
Pathé	Uproar in press. Case
Pres. out of vision	against butler dropped. End
	Judge's quote '...murder most foul'.

Note that the assembly script clearly describes what has to be said, not how to say it. The editor has plenty of latitude. For example, the suggested news footage from different sources might cut together in a number of different ways at different durations. A good editor might struggle to edit the vicar's interview and then suggest the speaker is so weak that his comments might better be included in the written commentary with some village exterior shots substituted. There may be a more appropriate place to sum up the village reactions at a later point in the story. What is imperative is that the director does not hand over a final written, or even worse a pre-recorded commentary for the editor to work from.

Writing the words

There will be probably several stages of picture editing.

1   A first assembly   The stage of trying to reproduce as far as possible the director's cutting script. At this stage there will probably be blanks for any musical sequences, montages may be missing and interviews left entire or edited very long. This is the stage for getting an idea of the structure and pace of the entire programme.

2   A rough cut   At this point the adjusted structure will appear, most sequences edited and included and obviously redundant material edited out. Titles and graphics will be missing and the programme still running over duration. This is the first stage where management or outsiders should be allowed a viewing.

3   The fine cut   The final programme cut to an exact duration complete with everything pictorial except

A word of warning

The world is turning digital fast. At the time of writing it is common for videotapes to be digitized prior to off-line editing. Since digitizing anything more than a brief news item is time consuming it is suggested that the director makes the main decisions about shots by running through rushes and digitizing only essential takes. The latest digital cameras even have a facility for electronically marking each take on location so that only those approved at the time will be digitized. This speeds up post production without any doubt. The trouble is that making television is not the same as canning beans. Speeding up the technical process has to take account of the human time for thought. Decisions taken on the spur of the moment often look wrong in the calm of the cutting room.

A presenter may have taken five attempts before getting, it seems, a satisfactory performance. It is dicing with death to immediately junk takes one to four. Take two may be fresher and only spoilt by a fluff of a word or two which will be covered by cutaway shots. Take five may have seemed perfect but the delivery sound tired, or a microphone may have crept into shot, or a distracting reflection appeared in a pair of spectacles. Shots which might appear quite redundant for the director's cutting order might become vital for extending or joining sequences later. The ability to distinguish the gold from the dross comes with experience. The director should be able to tell when something is really unusable, a disastrous interview, for example, but otherwise should keep hold of everything remotely useful.

This advice is quite useless of course for the sort of idiot who belongs to the 'if it moves, shoot it' school and returns from location with twenty times more footage than could ever be handled. One picture editor faced with mountains of tape by directors from a Yoof programme used to send the erring directors to the canteen, randomly throw half the cassettes in the bin, and tell the returning juveniles that there had been technical problems. Nobody noticed.

video effects and captions but with synchronous sound and music sequences. There may remain a lot of sound editing work still to do.

The terminology comes from film. Whatever the technology used the process remains much the same. The progress from an assembly up to the fine cut takes place during the video 'off-line' stage. This can take the editing through numerous generations of videotape in non-digital systems. With film the fine cut goes off to a laboratory with the original negative footage for 'neg cutting'. After this, further picture changes are no longer possible. Sound is mixed at a sound dubbing theatre. With video the fine cut is arrived at during the 'on-line'. The 'on-line' can be the place for bringing together video effects, putting on captions and grading colour.

With video adjustments to pictures as well as sound can be continued up to the last moment. On-line editing though is an expensive business and changes ought to be kept to a minimum. It is not the place for sudden second thoughts. It is only with the fine cut completed, that the commentary script should be written.

In many cases the director will write the commentary and the narration will be read by an actor or professional presenter. Very, very few directors or producers are much good at delivering commentaries, however well they write. Audiences react strongly to voices and draw all sorts of conclusions from them particularly in the absence of a face in vision. Reading a script is a dramatic performance. Accents and intonations count for a lot and a reader needs to be cast with great attention to programme content. So do not try to economize at the final stage of a programme by casting yourself as the out-of-vision narrator. Save that for your home videos. Programmes which strongly feature a reporter or presenter may use the same voice for out-of-vision commentary. A programme may be a personal view or 'one pair of eyes' report where this has to be the case. How far the reporter or presenter will write the final script will largely depend on how far he or she has been involved through the other stages of editing. Often a presenter will confidently leave the main writing to the director and make small adjustments before the sound recording. A professional actor might expect a completely finalized script and have no contact with the production prior to turning up to deliver the words.

The final shot list

It could seem logical to sit down with the fine cut in the editing suite and write the commentary bit by bit to the pictures. This is a clumsy and time consuming way of going about things and is hardly going to produce any literary gems. In a report from a war zone editing the pictures and writing and recording commentary may have to be done at the same time. Hard news reporting is different from anything else. Writing is best done undisturbed away from the edit suite and with notes or reference material to hand. The use of VHS cassettes with time code in vision has taken away a lot of the problems about writing words to pictures. It is possible to sit at home with a cassette of the fine cut to write and rewrite the words until they fit the picture sequences. If the commentary is to be brief and largely limited to linking sections of synchronous sound this might be an effective way of working. But if narration plays a significant role there is a better way of doing things. It may sound difficult but with a little practice it is both simple and effective.

1   Take a detailed shot list of the fine cut. It is only necessary to shot list those sections where commentary is needed, but such sections need to be described in great detail. Unlike the shot list for the first assembly this one is for the eyes of the writer only so a director may develop a personal shorthand. The information should be along the lines of something like this.

The Library Affair

Time	Shot
16.22	Synch. interview Policeman.
	In 'one of the mysteries...'
	out '...role of the Duke himself.'
	Stops talking 17.00
	turns to photograph of governess
17.02	Castle entrance exterior. Music begins.
17.08	CU gate house.

17.12	CU roses tilt up to coat of arms.
17.17	WA castle and grounds pan to ruined East wing.
17.22	Mix to newspaper headline fire. Zoom to photograph.
17.30	Mix to photo young Duke. Zoom to eyes 17.35.
17.40	Mix to interview Duke today.
17.42	Duke speaks synch.
	In 'Nobody could ever forget...'
	out '...the charred body.'
18.01	Church bell ringers interior. Speak at 18.03.
18.06	CUs bells in belfry. fx.
18.10	WA church and churchyard. Fade sound.
	Start commentary at 18.12.
18.15	Montage family graves.
18.25	Presenter walks into vision.
18.30	Leans on gravestone. Speaks at 18.32.
	In 'It's this particular grave that may hold...'

Writing such a list from beginning to end may be a chore but the writer now has no reason to look at the tape again until the first draft of the script is written and ready to be checked against the pictures. Note that the imaginary shot list above includes all sorts of clues to the words to be written. It is important to give the in and out cues for recorded interviews of recorded pieces to camera by the presenter. A well-written script will make back references to some shots and lead into others. For example in our opening interview with the policeman the picture editor has not brutally cut at the last word but left the interviewee contemplating a photograph. The incoming commentary might take the hint and begin, 'Mary the governess was not the only victim at the Castle...' The Duke is introduced by a slow mix from a portrait if his earlier self. The narration might like to lead into his opening words with something like 'Fifty years on the memory is vivid...' At this point make a note about music and effects. The sequence of the Duke cuts to the village bellringers and probably introduce the importance of the castle to the village community. This opens a new chapter and the picture editor has marked it by an abrupt charge in sound and pictures.

The viewers need a second or two to take in the change. There is no point in trying to speak over the sound of pealing bells. The pictures set the scene without needing words, only when we go to the graveyard and the bells are distant should the narrator start talking about the many generations buried there. As the writer will be familiar with the content of the story and the fine cut there is no point in shot listing anything not essential to cueing the commentary. There will though be places where the commentary must fit the pictures precisely. When the camera pans to the ruins of the east wing the commentary will have to match that point exactly and use it to lead into the newspaper story of the fire. It will be no good to be still rambling on about the family coat of arms. With a well-composed shot list a commentary almost writes itself.

> ### Trick of the trade
> There is no need to keep rewinding to the video cassette to check timings or to use a stop watch with the shot list. Both are perfectly acceptable ways of operating but a quicker way is to write the script on the basis that there are normally three words to every second of commentary. In the example there are fifteen seconds of exteriors of the castle and grounds before we pan to the scene of the fire. That means that the writer has a generous forty five words to set the scene and advance the story. There are thirteen seconds to talk about the gravestones, therefore a maximum of thirty nine words of commentary. The method is surprisingly accurate and seems to work just as well in many languages as well as English. The word count represents a maximum for the time available. Commentary need not rattle on from beginning to end. Pictures should be allowed to 'breathe' and establish themselves on screen. A well-read commentary should leave space for dramatic pauses. If in doubt under- rather than overwrite.

Fifteen easy lessons

1   Your commentary is there to supplement the pictures not to over-ride them. Do not describe what the pictures make perfectly obvious. Do not show us a typical English country churchyard and tell us 'Here in this typical English country graveyard.'

The first thing to learn about writing for television is when to shut up.

2   Use short sharp sentences and avoid qualifying and subordinate clauses. Punchy simple sentences are more memorable than long ones and are easier to fit accurately to pictures. Every sentence need not be beautifully constructed. This is writing for speaking not reading. In colloquial English phrases can be left to stand alone. 'Saint Birinus Church. Bell-ringing practice. Generation on generation of villagers buried together under this turf. But here a rather chilling gravestone. Not with others in a family plot. Far apart and half forgotten..., etc.

3   English has by far the largest vocabulary of any European language. Choose short words rather than long ones, Saxon ones rather than Latin. Short words more easily fit fleeting images. Polysyllables are often clumsy to read at the commentary recording.

4   Avoid jargon. Most jargon is designed as a shorthand for communication amongst small groups of people sharing a common interest. Television itself is a case in point. It would be unwise to assume that anyone not in the programme making business knows the difference between a track and a zoom let alone linear and non-linear, Steenbeck and Avid, LS and MCU. So as a political commentator don't introduce terms like OECD, UNWRA, UNESCO, ODA, FCO and so on without explaining them. There are some groups who take refuge in jargon as a means of impressing their peers whilst masking an underlying paucity of thought. Media studies provides a rich vein of portentous gobbledegook. Don't inflict any of this on the viewers. They can't pause to try to work out what you are getting at. Outside the realms of higher mathematics and symbolic logic what can't be clearly explained in clear English is not worth explaining.

5   Avoid lists and complex statistics. If the argument cannot be sustained without reference to trade figures, exchange rates, share prices or the like use graphics, make the graphics as clear and simple as possible, and calculate for them to be on screen long enough for the viewer to read them twice over.

6   Immediately cue the first appearance of new faces or changes of scene in the commentary. Do not come to a strange portrait and write 'one of the main actors in the dramatic events, here painted by Sir James Sargent, was the thirteenth Duke, Robert Ffanshawe'. You might get away with a florid style (just about) on the page but the poor viewer will be stuck looking at an unknown portrait and admiring the frame. Better to write 'Robert Ffanshawe the thirteenth Duke was one of the main players in these dramatic events. In this portrait by Sir James Sargent...' (but is it important to know who painted him? Is Sargent an important figure in the story or is this superfluous information? If we introduce Sargent is he well known or do we need to explain that he was a fashionable Society painter?)

7   Do not try to talk over dramatic sounds or the beginning of music (see our bellringers above). If there are dramatic sound effects, a gun firing, a door slamming, or a lion roaring then write a pause in the commentary. The desire to fill up every second with endless verbiage is the mark of the inept corporate video. It can also be a consequence of attempting to write the commentary first and squeeze in pictures to fit afterwards.

8   Do not write using acronyms and figures. Do not write 'the UN' but 'The United Nations' not 'in the year 1997' but 'the year nineteen ninety-seven'. This is the way it will be read from the script in the recording. It also is a check against unexplained jargon and underestimated timings. Write using 'can't', 'don't', 'won't', etc. not 'cannot', 'do not', or 'will not'. Write for the ear not the page.

9   Do not write commentary so tightly that the reader must gabble to keep up. Make cues a fraction early so that the reader can draw breath before actually speaking. Once a well-paced delivery with dramatic pauses is rehearsed the commentary is often found to be longer than when the director was reading his own words.

10   If the reader is neither the director nor programme presenter the production office should send out a copy of the commentary script and a cassette of the fine cut well in advance. The timings and editorial content may remain sacrosanct, but it is hard to write for another

voice. A professional presenter will be able to suggest turns of phrase better suited to his or her own delivery. Even actors sometimes find difficulties with certain combinations of words and will advise changing them. There should always be time for incorporating corrections of text before going to the commentary booth. It wastes expensive time and wrecks delivery if there have to be many pauses and rewrites.

11   Don't repeat yourself. Do not write as a link 'The general appeared on the balcony and warned the demonstrators to disperse in five minutes or he would open fire'. If we cut to a general appearing on a balcony and shouting to a crowd of demonstrators 'I give you five minutes to disperse or I will open fire!' Duplicating the same information in introductory links and recorded presentation is a frequent and often hilarious fault of news programmes.

12   Always tell the viewers something new. Don't provide portentous waffle to describe the obvious or fill time. Natural history commentary writers seem particularly prone to the redundant cliché. How many hundred times have you heard the phrase 'At last the rains come' to accompany storm clouds, lightening, thunderclaps and an out-of-frame bucket of water dribbling over parched earth, or 'Eat or be eaten, only the strong survive in the eternal struggle...' As yet another hyena disembowels yet another wildebeest. Tell the viewer what cannot be deduced from the pictures. Tell us about the crushing force of the hyena's jaws, anything special about its teeth or digestive system, whether the wildebeest ever wins, or if either species is getting scarcer. How many inches of rain fall in an hour? Where does it come from? How do the clouds build up? Why do they have strange anvil shapes? Does the commentary need to say anything at all or is it just there in the hope of keeping the viewers awake or padding out the shots?

13   Never send a written commentary script for clearance to a client, sponsor, or any television executive unless a question of law or taste is in question. The safest technique is to do a 'scratch' commentary recording with your own voice onto a cassette and write a note

emphasizing the impossibility of altering the timings. In almost every case the outsider will both want to change sections and, more dangerously, add masses of superfluous information over any pictures not already smothered in words. A brilliant television commentary read without pictures can look sketchy, ungrammatical and be scarcely intelligible. A commentary which reads on the page as a brilliant magazine article is probably overwritten and even incomprehensible in the context of television.

14   Do not forget the impact of humour and irony. These can be written or conveyed by the delivery. Dull-as-ditchwater commentaries and deadpan deliveries with no change of mood or pace soon bore a viewer to death.

15   Do not turn up at a recording with a scruffy single copy of the script. The reader, the sound engineer, the picture editor and anyone else involved will need copies. Make sure that the cues and timings are clearly marked in the left-hand column. Do not let sentences run over from page to page and use a large typeface. On-line suites and dubbing theatres can be dimly lit places. Try to type the copy for the reader on a soft paper. Many a commentary recording has been slowed up or ruined by the sound of paper rustles and page turns in front of the microphone.

> **Trick of the trade**
> There are places in commentary where the words have to end at a precise spot either to make way for an abrupt change of scene, a sudden sound effect, a music cue or whatever. Rather than take timings from the beginning of the sequence it is easier to take a timing backwards from the critical moment in question.

When looking at a cut sequence of pictures and a mountain of possible information to include in a commentary script, repeatedly ask yourself the questions:

1   What precise information must I impart here?
2   What general information could I put in there?
3   Do I need to open my mouth at all?

10

The sound of music

There never was a silent cinema. From the beginning of motion pictures the audience felt uneasy with watching images in silence except for the clatter of a projector. The immediate answer was to have an accompanying pianist and then later a small musical ensemble. Before long entire pit orchestras were engaged and special scores circulated. The eve of the talkies was a golden age for the mighty Wurlitzer theatre organ which combined musical scores with a wondrous array of sound effects from horses hooves to slapsticks, church bells and gun shots. It is impossible to think of television devoid of music. Yet many a director and producer has come to devoutly wish it could be so. Dealing with music can be like trying to tap dance through a minefield.

Music can come from many sources:

- Music recorded on location
- Specially composed and recorded scores
- Commercial recordings
- Pre-recorded library 'mood' music
- Rehearsed musical performances

Each needs approaching in quite different ways, and each is liable to quite distinct sets of problems.

Location recordings

Music is all around us. Documentaries benefit enormously from music which arises naturally from the action or is integral to a location. It would be difficult or perverse to make a documentary about Mexico City without hearing Mariachi music. Buskers are (illegally) much a part of the London Underground. Dress shops are afflicted by booming rock, Irish pubs by fiddles. This is without counting carnival scenes, parades and parties. Few things do more to create a sense of location and the mood of a scene than the use of incidental music. Recording music on location is not easy. Editing music can be wildly time consuming. The problem is frequently how to get rid of unwanted background music as much as recording music that might be wanted.

Shooting

Music requires a professional recordist. It is a waste of time trying to cover anything involving music with a one-man crew using a microphone strapped on top of the camera. Although the eye and the brain accept picture cuts the ear will reject any simultaneous cuts in music. The simplest rhythm or melody has its own structure. Whilst words are infinitely flexible it is almost impossible to chop a section out of a piece of music without causing pain to a listener. It follows that the location director has a simple choice.

Either record as much continuous music as possible in one continuous take and subsequently look for extra shots which might be edited with the sound track, or get rid of the music entirely during the shooting but record it separately later. The pictures and music track can be recombined in post production. If edited dialogue with background music is involved the latter is the only satisfactory solution.

Unwanted location music is the curse of the picture editor. A simple scene might be the concourse of a railway terminus. Railway stations carefully select their piped music. During the rush hour they may deliberately pick tracks with a marching rhythm to speed things up. During delays something more restful might be appropriate. There is the added complication in interruptions by the station announcer. Any attempt to cut together shots of trains, crowds, faces, and whatever with original synchronous sound will be chaotic, on each cut the background acoustic will be different. Each music cut will have a different rhythm in a different key and often a different tune, trains will apparently be thundering past behind one shot and suddenly vanish in the next, the station announcement will come and go as disconnected strangled yelps between sequences. If a significant amount of location dialogue is wanted the first move must be to ask the railway authorities if they would stop the piped music during the recording time. This is something to ask at the recce. There is no time to bluff your way through on the shooting day. If they refuse all is not lost. Remember the wide shot, mid-shot, tight shot mantra. Set up the camera in position for the best wide shot. Check with the recordist that the ambient sound is satisfactory. Sticking the microphone next to a public address loudspeaker or pointing at a throbbing diesel locomotive will not help. Record continuously at least twice as much sound as you are likely to need. To be safe take a complete four- or five-minute music track. A clearly discernible musical start or finish can be a boon in post production. If you have the advantage of shooting on film the recordist can keep going and the camera can cut as the operator wishes. With videotape it is vital that the camera keeps running whether it stays on the static wide shot, pans about looking for close-ups or even is left looking at the ground. Next go for the available mid-shots and tight shots, either from the same camera set-up or various other positions.

Finally go for 'buzz tracks' of close-up sounds for whatever has been seen on the earlier shots. If trains have been seen revving up and departing try to record the sound of one doing just that. Carriage doors slamming, feet marching up steps, turnstiles clicking, anything seen in mid-shot or close-up needs close-up sound, and plenty of it. The picture editor now has the material to lay down a continuous uninterrupted music track and mix in the special location sound effects. If there must be dialogue try to do it in the quietest spot using a directional microphone as close as possible and pointing away from the main sources of background noise. This advice holds good even for backgrounds which sound either constant or plainly repetitive. A ceremony at a Hindu temple might apparently involve ten or fifteen minutes of a repetitious chant 'Hare Krishna, Hare Krishna, Krishna Krishna, Hare, Hare', etc. The temptation is to wave the camera about, stopping and starting, grabbing pictures of musicians, devotees, garlanded statues, priests and all. With all the activity the pictures and music ought to edit painlessly together. Do not be deceived. The mantra will imperceptibly accelerate, the rhythms on the tabla become increasingly complex, the key of the chanting will change and the order of the words may swap. The director may start by being ignorant about Indian music but is going to learn fast when later none of the pictures cut with the music. The same advice applies as with the railway station. Keep calm. Shoot twice as much as you are likely to need in a continuous take as soon as possible. Try to include a distinct starting or end point. Then go for all the extra close shots you can get.

One solution to getting both a continuous useful music track with enough close-up pictures would be to ask for the same music to be repeated twice or more. There may be practical reasons why this may not be possible. The temple devotees are not likely to repeat their devotions just for a camera. A request for repeat renditions can lead to additional trouble.

Words of warning
Most musicians belong to a Trade Union. Even cathedral choirs and regimental bands do. Assuming even that no copyrights are infringed the director will get away with shooting documentary footage about these. But once the director requests anything special, like the repeat of a passage or a rearrangement of the programme order, it counts as a directed performance. The musicians will demand to be paid. A military band adds up to an awful lot of individual Musicians Union fees.

Handy hint
A musical group might agree to repeat the same piece. The temptation will be to shoot the first continuous performance as a wide master shot to go with the sound and then use the second rendition to look for close-ups. In fact no two performances will be precisely identical. In some musical forms like jazz there may be wide variations. Disparities are most apparent in close-ups, spectacularly so if vocalists are involved. So it makes sense to go for as many close-ups as possible during the first master recording. Save the wide shots for the second performance where the disparities with the master music recording will be less obvious.

Close-ups will not work if musicians are obviously playing a different section, a choir is mouthing different words, percussion has changed rhythm or a conductor is waving his baton irrelevantly. Assuming it is for a documentary context and not an actual musical recital there are tricks which help to deceive the viewers.

1   Get a very wide shot with plenty of depth. From the back of the temple with devotees silhouetted in the foreground and the altar in the far distance. A picture from behind musicians with the conductor or other orchestral sections in the background. Get as much continuous footage as possible, ideally including each section of the orchestra and each soloist in distant action. So long as it is unclear what music is being played continuity will not be critical. Of course a conductor will have to be addressing the same section of the orchestra in adjacent shots, a percussionist cannot be seen flailing around in one shot and looking at his fingernails in the immediate next one. A slow track around the backs of the performers can look very good in this context, overhead shots make great cutaways. Audience shots are always safe.

2   Remember an awkwardly large number of viewers are familiar with music and musical instruments. To fool them get the maximum number of cutaways which avoid showing the keys of the instruments. Close-ups of wind players can be shot so that the breathing of the players is plain but the finger work is not. Brass instruments offer possibilities for reflection shots which look impressive but do clearly reveal the musicians. Guitars can be shot at angles which do not show the fret board. If shooting a piano always get shots looking over the top of the instrument but hiding the hands on the keyboard. Shooting over a grand piano can produce a range of impressive shots; only inappropriate shoulder positions will give the game away. Go for what are in effect reaction shots and cutaways; music sheets being turned, close-ups of faces, extreme low or high angles, big close-ups of batons, big profiles of reed players, organ pipes or stained glass windows, pints of beer or bottles of rum in the foreground. Whatever the location suggests.

Sod's Law dictates that:

1   You never have enough shots to edit even the briefest musical item.

2   The camera operator will get overexcited and not hold any of the shots long enough for them to be of use. No shot should be held for less than six seconds; ten or over is better. Unplanned panning and zooming shots will be useless.

Words of warning

Music is subject to a complex web of rights. The same piece may be subject to separate rights in the tune, the lyrics, the arrangement, the recording and the performance. For a more detailed description of the problems see the companion volume *The Essential Television Handbook*. Background music or music in brief snatches incidental to the action is covered by the idea of 'fair dealing' and not likely to attract attention. But television generally is becoming obsessed by enforcing rights and playing fast and loose with other people's music is going to bring down the wrath of the several copyright protection societies. Copyright is being extended from 50 to 70 years under European legislation. Even tunes like 'Happy Birthday To You' are copyright protected. Problems can arise in the strangest places. A ceremony in Bogotá, capital of Colombia, is the sunset lowering of the national flag. This is performed by an honour guard of officer cadets dressed in pre-1914 Prussian uniforms who march to the main square from the military academy. As the band marches in it strikes up a teutonic rendition of 'Yellow Submarine'. There is copyright in both the music and the arrangement for German marching bands. It is unlikely that even the Beatles would take on the Colombian Army over their choice of music. But the same latitude may not be given to a documentary broadcast in the United Kingdom. If a director tries to construct a brilliant opening or closing sequence cut to this 'Yellow Submarine' it will certainly not be counted as fair dealing and legal action will follow. Better wait to record the National Anthem later in the ceremony. That at least will be in the public domain.

Library music

As a general rule commercial recordings are to be avoided by the programme maker. Most American recordings are in effect impossible to clear for rights, and most recent European ones can only be cleared with great difficulty and frequently at prohibitive expense. The problems are explored at length in *The Essential Television Handbook*. What the director is left with is a copious selection of specially recorded music which is guaranteed clearable. There are over sixty music libraries affiliated to the Mechanical Copyright Protection Society providing tens of thousands of tracks ranging from two- or three-second musical stings for commercials to versions of classical symphonies. Groups of performers are frequently disguised by fanciful names. Sometimes they are ad hoc bunches of session musicians, sometimes well-known groups or orchestras. Tracks and albums often have wildly misleading titles. 'Rebel Attack', 'Executive Breakdown' or 'Zoos for Twos' may contain themes evoking almost anything. The only answer is to plough through as many records as possible to find something suitable for your purpose. Thankfully everything is now issued on compact disc and skipping through tracks is quite fast. Library music is not free. There is a scale of charges depending on the nature of the transmission and the extent of rights applied for. Worldwide clearance for a thirty second commercial can cost over £1500. At the other end of the scale rights for an in-house corporate video can cost less than £20 for up to thirty seconds. All music tracks are supposed to be cleared and paid for before transmission. Failure to do so can incur financial penalties and in blatant cases may result in legal action. The MCPS and the other copyright protection societies are extremely active so it is dangerous to slip in a bit of library background music and hope that nobody will notice. Assuming rights are cleared there is the difficulty of fitting the pictures and music together.

Never cut the pictures first and then try to play in music second. Always start with the sound track and then fit the pictures to the music. Music by definition has its own form and rhythms. So does any skilfully edited film or video sequence. If the rhythm of the music bears no relationship to the cutting of the pictures the result will be irritation. Music demands the attention of the listener. Irrelevant music burbling in the background instantly distracts from the power of the pictures and words. The idea that a dull story can be improved or extended by 'putting a bit of music over it' is a complete misconception. It is a misconception encouraged by less than competent videotape editors, however. Sound editing can be much more of a problem than cutting pictures. A bit of irrelevant music can look a tempting way for papering over mistakes.

The commonest uses of music are in montages of still pictures, often as title sequences, live action sequences in film commercials and music promos, and documentary sequences evoking landscape and mood. In an ideal world all these would be carefully worked out and storyboarded before shooting commences. With commercials this is almost always the case. Music used in a documentary context rarely leaves this option. The director may decide to evoke the grandeur of a cathedral by cutting shots of the architecture to suitable music. But the exact piece may not have been chosen by the day of the shoot or be dependent on organ music recorded on site. The choice of shots must depend on the inspiration of the camera operator and director at the time. The editing order will have to be created entirely in the editing suite. In consequence the director is going to need very many shots in a very great variety. The pace of the music will dictate the pace of the cutting; rhythms impose cutting points. Unless images are going to be thrown about at random the cutting will have a logical structure, which means that perfectly good images may not find a place and have to be junked. A 30-second item cut to an upbeat music track will need the director to provide a selection of at least 50 or 60 potentially useful shots. Music eats up pictures. Try counting the number and duration of shots used in a film commercial which has been cut to music. Music has obvious logical starting and stopping points. A very common mistake made by beginners is to turn up at an edit with a full 60-second music track, enough pictures for ten seconds, and a request for the sequence to run at 20.

Music that just fades away at the end of a sequence is always unsatisfactory, attempts to edit lumps out of the middle of a track often results in the aural equivalent of dropping a brick on the listener's foot. There will be readers who will not see the point of any of this. Many people have practically no musical or rhythmic sense. Everyone likes to think that they have but one glance at an English dance floor will reveal the fallacy of that one. This may not be an insurmountable problem if this is so. The selection of music can be delegated to someone else, frequently an enthusiastic picture editor, who is not afflicted by tin ears.

> **Handy hint**
> There are times when a director may go out with a preselected music track. It might be the intention to cut images of an exotic market to a vibrant local rhythm. The editing will be much easier, and fun, if the market occupants unselfconsciously move to the music. It is a help to take along a powerful audio cassette player and a recording of the chosen track. People walking, children playing and even stallholders chopping up meat or stacking vegetables will find it hard not to pick up the beat. Even if the idea is to evoke sailing ships at sunset a cassette of the music is useful. Slow music sequences are a proper place for slow pans and zooms with slow dissolves between shots. As the speed of camera moves can be critical it will be more than helpful if the camera operator can listen to the music and get a feel of its pace.

Music hints

1   Do not always be obvious or literal in a choice of music. There is no special merit in selecting 'White Cliffs of Dover' for shots of ferry boats or 'Carnival of the Animals' for a zoo sequence just because the titles fit. A sequence about steam trains should not send the director straight to 'Coronation Scot'. A well chosen tabla and sitar section from an Indian raga may be more effective.

2   Be very careful about selecting very well-known music. Music has strong personal connotations for many people. This can be particularly dangerous where a piece is already been used on film. Anyone who has seen Disney's *Fantasia* will find it impossible to hear 'The Sorcerer's Apprentice' without thinking of Mickey Mouse. Bach's *Toccata and Fugue* might conjure up a baroque church to the director but flash up images of a Hammer Horror film in the minds of others.

3   Rubbish music does not enhance a sequence, it demeans it. The mark of truly awful corporate videos is an insistence of plastering irrelevant repetitious music from start to finish over the sound track (and not uncommonly non-stop commentary over the

music!). Shots of a power boat race do not gain anything from being cut to repetitious percussion. Slushy strings throughout a promotional video on a machine tool factory is just a sign that the recordist and picture editor were not up to their jobs. Crashing bars of rock music do not disguise a lousy picture edit or terrible camera shots. They just make sure that nobody can miss them.

4   Do not be afraid to pick music to counterpoint rather than literally interpret the pictures. A Hell's Angel motor cycle rally might suggest heavy metal rock music but would gain different connotations if cut to

1. 'The Ride of the Valkyries' by Wagner
2. A requiem mass
3. The ballad 'Hit The Road Jack' or
4. 'The Teddy Bear's Picnic'

5   Use music for humorous as well as dramatic purposes. It is a powerful weapon. It can though be used in a defamatory manner. A broadcast holiday programme decided to accompany criticism of a travel company's accommodation with the theme music from the prison camp escape series *The Colditz Story*. They were obliged to pay damages. The danger of playing any music that comes to hand over dull pictures was illustrated in one Commonwealth country when a director decided to pep up a news story of the arrival of the Head of State by spinning in a background disc. The theme was of the ballad 'Olé, I am the bandit'.

6   Never continue music from a picture sequence over an interview. When someone is speaking to camera we want to hear them alone. Hollywood style drama may use musical underscoring with melodramatic dialogue but this is specially composed and recorded material. Conversely when going from dialogue to music lead with the music shortly before the picture cut.

Commissioned music

The current range of library music should more than suffice in the search for good opening or closing title sequences and brief musical interludes. Problems arise if the director plans to underscore long sequences. Mood music has to be just that, appropriate background which enhances mood. A disc of library music may contain a couple of good theme tracks but become irritatingly repetitious if track after track has to be pressed into service. Mixing tracks from different recordings can destroy any unifying musical style. A solution is to specially commission and record your own music. This has been the answer in the cinema since the birth of the talkies. (As with television today the earliest film music tracks were often used to cover the inadequacies of primitive synchronous sound recordings.) Specially composed music used to be regarded as out of the question for all but the most prestigious television programmes. It was a case of library music or nothing. Today things are going very much in the other direction. There are three reasons.

1 New technology means that very creditable tracks can be recorded very cheaply and simply. A commissioned track can work out no more expensive than library music.

2 Internationalization of television has resulted in an evident increase in the British use of background music. What was once the preserve of costume dramas is now common in dramatized documentaries, natural history programmes, science and history, comedy and education.

3 Copyright has become a bitterly fought-over battleground. The only way of ensuring total world rights and exclusive use for your music is to have it specially commissioned and recorded.

Before rushing off to sign up a symphony orchestra and approach a renowned conductor pause to consider the problems. They all involve money.

How much music do you really need?

The longer the tracks the more recording sessions will be needed. The longer the recording sessions the larger the payments for both players and technical facilities. A programme does not necessarily benefit from having music wall to wall.

What Musicians Union agreements cover your particular programme?

The MU has detailed agreements for the PACT independent companies, the BBC, satellite, closed circuit and even CD ROM. Payments may vary according to whether both title themes and background music are recorded at a single session. Programmes in a series may be counted as individual productions. If they are the players might be entitled to payment per programme, even if backgrounds for more than one episode are played in a single recording session or identical music is played in two episodes.

How many musicians do you need?

This is something to discuss early on with the composer but the director ought to start with an idea at least as to what is possible. A solo instrumentalist is obviously going to be less of a problem than a big band. A guitarist might double up on lute and banjo. A saxophonist might play both oboe and clarinet. Often a guitar and clarinet can be preferable to a huge orchestration. Some of the biggest turkeys in big budget drama on British TV in the 1990s have been distinguished by wildly over-the-top music tracks.

Can you use synthesizers and electronic means to dispense with players?

Well up to a point. The Musicians Union is very aware that a couple of musicians multitracking with a range of instruments and using synthesizers could substitute for a small orchestra. There are detailed agreements in force. On the other hand an amazing range of music can be generated on a single synthesizer and even student productions can now attempt ambitious musical scores.

At the bottom line exactly how much of the budget can be devoted to the music?

Unexpected music bills can cripple a budget. Once committed the director cannot just panic and stop because the costs start mounting. At a certain point it is in for a penny, in for a pound. The first person to talk to is the composer. Agree the music budget and stick to it. The composer needs to be fully involved throughout the production process.

Working with the composer

1   As soon as possible explain the content and intention of the production. If the composer knows from the outset that, for instance, the project is a documentary about a war and will involve scenes of battle, scenes of desolation, episodes at sea or in a desert he or she can start thinking of suitable themes and arrangements.

2   Bring the composer to the editing suite as soon as the picture editor has a satisfactory assembly. With factual programmes the music will probably be appropriate only for specific segments. Music under talking heads may be normal in American soaps but irritates in factual programmes. The presence of music can alter the pacing of the picture cutting. If our notional war documentary involves shots of a convoy at sea three of four selected archive shots cut quickly together might suffice for the commentary. With additional music there may be space for twice as many shots, or for the same three or four to be held on screen for twice the time. Music can be an antidote to the words-first obsession of journalist directors. The picture editor has to know where there is an opportunity for breathing spaces where pictures and music can be left to work their magic without commentary.

3   Ask the composer to submit a demo tape of the main themes as early as possible. Most composers use electronic equipment that can convey a pretty good impression of what the final arrangement will sound like. The director and composer may have rather different ideas about the pace and mood of the music and this is the time to argue the point.

4   You are very unlikely to have the luxury of an orchestra and conductor in a huge recording studio playing to a projected fine cut of your masterpiece as during the heyday of Hollywood. Remember the rule that in editing the music comes first and the pictures are best cut to the recorded music. Ideally the music should be recorded and in the picture editor's hands well before the final cut. However good the overall timing

it is unlikely that the music will precisely match the picture cuts if it is just added in at the sound dub. Sophisticated digital 'sampling' techniques do enable music to be stretched and manipulated to fit. Music speed can be altered without also altering the pitch. Like so many electronic miracles sampling is best considered as a useful last resort and not an alternative to getting things right in the first place, only sophisticated dubbing suites are equipped with the appropriate facilities and it takes time and money.

5   Music is not easily rushed. The composer needs time to work out and agree the main themes, to write the score and to copy the parts for the musicians prior to the recording session which itself has to be before the film fine cut and track laying or video sound dub on line. In other words music greatly complicates the production planning. It needs care and is never something to leave to the last minute.

Word of warning

Even for a student video the composer must provide original compositions and arrangements. The temptation to employ a friend with a synthesizer or a couple of local rock musicians to compose and play might not fall foul of Musicians Union regulations. What will create a furore is if the composer happily incorporates tunes or themes which are somebody else's copyright. Established composers often sail close to the wind with arrangements that sound remarkably akin to familiar modem classics or pop tunes. The recent vogue for pop musicians to 'sample' tracks from other recordings has complicated matters. Disputes have started arriving in the courts. Film composers have always played with all sorts of musical references in their scores but if this goes as far as blatantly lifting tunes without first clearing copyright there will be trouble.

Performing to playback

Not uncommonly a director will want to go to location with actors, dancers or musical performers to shoot a sequence to playback. Pop promo videos are the obvious example as are music driven commercials. There are many others including dance routines, comedy sketches and arts programmes. If the performers are an established group there may be a choreographer. If not the director will have to attend rehearsals, break down the musical score and probably storyboard the musical number. A professional choreographer works as a professional equal with the director. Dance is one area where a top quality video monitor in essential on set. For shooting to playback the director will need:

1   A master sound track. If there is any music editing or sound manipulation to be done it must be carried out prior to preparing the track. The master track stays with the picture editor.

2   A fully synchronous duplicate track to be played on location.

3   Means to record the performance and the playback sound track together.

Old film equipment will require the playback track to be specially prepared with an electronic pulse by a facility house so the quarter inch record and playback machines might stay synchronous with each other and the master in the cutting room. The synchronized playback tape is switched so as to slave the record machine. Quarter inch tape might appear to run at always the same speed but machines vary and a recording may drift disastrously out of synchronism in less than a minute, which is disastrous when singers appear in close-up. Fortunately good quality digital audio tape (DAT) recorders are incredibly reliable. Far from drifting out of synchronism at several frames a minute they can hold synchronism for up to half an hour and only stray a few frames overall. As a single camera shoot will break down into a number of short takes the director will probably get away with just this. With video the playback will use a videotape prerecorded with the same time code as the master.

Whatever the equipment there must be loud enough amplification for the entire company to hear and perform. Thereafter the procedure is simple. The recordist plays the duplicate master tape and the artists mime. The record tape covers the picture and also gathers as good a location sound as possible. The picture editor will need the location sound as a guide to select the correct pictures to be slotted into the master sound recording. As elsewhere the pictures are the slaves to the music.

Handy hint

All performers whether dancers, vocalists or actors have difficulty in picking up a mime from a cold start. Always give a good musical run up to the beginning of each section so they can pick up the rhythm before leaping into action. If the shot is to begin hard after a silence or at the beginning it is best for the director to give a loud verbal count in for a few bars. As with all drama and movement always overlap sound and action at the beginning and end of sequences. Even if you know you intend to cut hard on a particular beat you do no help dancers or musicians by shouting 'Cut!' at the particular editing point. Let the artists perform good long sections at a time.

11
Performance

Sooner or later every director will be faced with music in one form or other. Most of the examples so far described involve music being used in the service of non-music programmes. Music direction reaches its most challenging when a musical performance is itself the subject. Pop, jazz, orchestral, opera, ballet, chamber or folk, the genres are irrelevant. The problems are the same. The main difference is the scale of the performance. There will be a lot more to shooting a complete performance of Stravinsky's 'Rite of Spring' or a full-blown rock concert in a stadium than a

Figure 11.1

vocalist with keyboard accompaniment or a pair of folk singers in a studio.

There is no point in thinking of shooting a performance on single camera. Performance needs multiple cameras and plenty of them. Directors of rock concerts in particular use multi camera outside broadcast scanners but in addition have numbers of free-range ISO cameras roaming about to get the back-stage and on-stage close-ups otherwise unobtainable. Just remember that this material will have to be edited.

This book began by warning of the potential problems caused by shooting a simple interview on two ISO single cameras. Consider this in the context of a concert. One of our most distinguished documentary directors was faced with shooting Tchaikowsky's '1812' overture and, lacking OB experience, decided to shoot with a battery of film cameras. At the climax of the piece cannons roar and cymbals crash. Unfortunately at that moment the cameras were each busily looking elsewhere, pointing at each other, finding focus or changing magazines. The cymbalist's moment of glory had to be covered by a distant wide shot.

The success of multi camera largely depends on the professionalism of all the members of the crew. Music defies the one-man-and-his-dog cost cutting logic of our times. The best director will be sunk without a highly professional camera crew, excellent lighting, a brilliant vision mixer and a first rate PA.

Most television directors pass their entire careers without being called on to shoot a musical performance. Anyone without musical interests should avoid the idea. It is a very specialist area. If the occasion does arise, and you want to have a go, don't panic. With planning, always the key to studio or OB direction, you have a fair chance of doing a creditable job.

There are many different musical styles, all demanding different ways of lighting and shooting. No two directors will ever arrive at the same shots for the same performance. Musical direction is not a matter of managing to get cameras pointing the right way at the right time. It is a matter of personal interpretation.

What goes for a folk ballad does not go for heavy metal rock. A jazz quartet and a concert string quartet are similar but demand subtly different treatment. There are two different environments facing the music director: studio and outside broadcast. There are two different recording situations: recorded or live performance. There are a number of possible permutations within these.

Recorded music

The situation is much as described in the previous chapter dealing with shooting performances to playback. It is a matter of applying multicamera techniques to artists who mime to playback. It is the easiest way to record pop and rock groups and for the director has enormous advantages. The recording will be commercially available and can be listened to as many times as the director wants in the preparation of a camera script without even setting eyes on the group.

The lighting supervisor can set up an appropriate rig and the designer create a workable set for the numbers and style of performance. So long as the director is capable of distinguishing the main instruments such as keyboard, drums, lead guitar, etc. and also find out where the instruments are usually positioned on the stage practically all the preparation can be done in advance. The duration of the piece and the performance will never change. Nobody is going to add extra bars or a new verse.

Live music

The problem with a live rendition is that things change. If the director makes plans on the basis of a commercial recording which is to be replicated it may be that a live studio version is very different. Commercial recordings have been 'got at' by the record company sound engineers. Concert performances vary and in the case of pop music evolve all the time. Lyrics get modified. Jazz is by definition improvisational.

Location shooting

Some location performances are planned with television cameras in mind. An outside broadcast from a cathedral is an example. In this case the director has almost as much control as in a studio with the advantage of being able to exploit the visual possibilities of the site. There is probably ample opportunity for rehearsal for both performers and cameras. In many cases however, the cameras are subordinate to the requirements of a paying audience. With a live concert the director will have very little control over the proceedings. There may be only one chance to get a camera rehearsal and then everything will happen very fast.

Studio live performances

At least here the director is working on home turf. The artists can be booked for adequate rehearsal time and the audience, if there is one, is also under the control of the studio. It is the best of all worlds for the director though not always the environment which gets the most sparkling performances from the artists. The director has a choice of direction techniques, one is strictly for the gung ho macho director of live programmes, the other for the true professional. Either:

1   You decide to direct by the seat of your pants and treat the concert like a deranged live sporting fixture. You busk it. You block in the basic shots with the camera crew and then improvise during the take. You may get away with this if the music is a predictable rock number. Even so you need to be able to count bars and preferably do your own vision mixing.

        You need to be familiar with the type of music. If you can't distinguish between lead and rhythm guitar, don't try rock. If you don't know a viola from a cello keep clear of chamber music. If you can't sense when a jazz soloist is going to repeat a riff or a chorus don't touch jazz. Editors of magazine programmes frequently fall for the happy idea of inviting all sorts of musical groups to a live studio without a thought for the unfortunate director. That is fine as a bit of fun or a means to 'play out' a programme under closing credits but can be musically awful.

Or:

2   The director ought to prepare a thorough camera script and makes any modifications during a

properly planned rehearsal period. The gung ho director is going to fall flat on his face sooner or later. The meticulous inexperienced director will not fail if the accepted procedures are kept to.

How to do it

1   Shooting instrumental music depends on the director being able to count bars. There is no substitute. It is not possible to try to time cuts to a stopwatch, even with the simple business of shooting to recorded music. In a live performance, even of a classical piece, the duration of different renditions will vary by several seconds over a few minutes. Cutting to stopwatch timings will just result in progressively worse early or late cuts.

Fortunately almost all popular music, even exotic ethnic styles, can be simplified to a simple four beats to the bar pattern. If you can count up to four you can direct most music.

2   The performance must not come as a surprise. The director needs any reference material available. If the number is a part of a commercial recording then getting a sound cassette is the first priority. A lot of pop and rock music is marketed with a promotional video. A lot of these may be fanciful creations but they can give a clue to the style of performance.

There may be a recorded videotape of an earlier concert or performance. If the music has not yet been commercially issued the group, or its manager, should still be able to get a tape to the director well in advance. If the director reads music a score is invaluable. Best of all will be a chance to attend a public performance by the musicians.

3   Make a sketch plan of the line-up. Most musical groups have a set line-up for players and instruments. The sections of orchestras have a fixed seating pattern. The director may need to make some adjustments for the studio settings but these should disturb the customary arrangements as little as possible.

A complication arises when artists move position

during the performance. Pop music soloists can be very mobile. Traditional jazz musicians may play different numbers with different instruments in different combinations. The director needs to sketch these. The information is vital for the camera script and also for lighting and set design.

4   Play the cassette of the number again and again until the music and the lyrics are totally familiar. Anyone who wants to be a television director has to be able to 'see' pictures in their heads. This is regardless of whether the subject is the music of Debussy or a documentary report. If the beginner lacks this inborn ability then the cruel but fair advice is to get out of television production. Listening to the music should leave the director with a mental picture of how the direction will look, even in cases when he or she has never set eyes on the performers.

Word of warning

Many a music director has risked a lynching through playing the same music again and again and again at work or home. The most solid office walls seem to turn to tissue paper when someone is subjected to incessantly repeated and interrupted passages of the same music. Few marriages will survive two days of this cruel treatment; only listen to your cassettes on earphones and at the lowest volume. Even then the middle of a field is safer than an office or railway carriage.

The script

Get hold of the words of lyrics and where applicable the score from the group or record company. Accuracy is everything in music direction. The lyrics of many pop songs are occasionally almost impossible to decipher from commercial recordings and are 'adolescent gibberish' when they can be decoded. Some musical items may be sung in an unfamiliar foreign language. This is not too much of a problem. Lyrics are a boon. A soloist gives the director something to hang onto and imposes an obvious pattern to the shooting. The lyrics ought to set the mood of the shooting, but however important the words may be the director should write the camera script according to the beat.

A first draft of a script should be written as shown below with the words and instrumental breaks written down the right half-of the page leaving the left half free for the camera shot descriptions and shot numbers.

8 BARS AND TWO BEATS TUTTI
DAMON
Don't know why
Don't know where
My baby's gone
Yeah
4 BARS LEAD GUITAR AND DRUMS
SONIA
She's away with the fairies
Etc., etc.

A problem to watch out for is that sometimes different people take up the vocals than on an earlier recording. If rehearsal time is limited the director needs to check for this. An unexpected change can knock a hole in the camera script and lead to the most glaring mistake, a cut during a solo to someone who is not singing.

The initial script illustrated above allows you now to mark your possible cutting points on the words of the lyrics along with the beginnings and ends of instrumental breaks. These will offer the most likely cutting points. The ends of musical bars are the next most obvious points. For those who are not particularly musical the easiest way to count bars is to call or tap them out aloud. So for a four bar instrumental break the director would count one-two-three four, two-two-three four, three-two-three four, four-two-three four. The breakdown bar by bar can be marked in pencil on the shooting script. (Note: do not use anything other than a soft pencil on a script. By the time you have changed your mind a couple of times using a pen it will look like a manic spider has been at work!)

Now the intro to 'Fairyland' will read

2 BARS DRUMS/
2 BARS SAXOPHONE/
2 BARS DRUMS AND KEYBOARDS/

2 BARS AND TWO BEATS TUTTI/
DAMON
Don't know why
Don't know where/
My baby's gone/
Yeah/
4 BARS LEAD GUITAR AND DRUMS/
SONIA
She's away with the fairies/
Etc., etc.

You will finish with a basic breakdown of the whole number. Before starting to think about actual camera shots there are a number of other considerations.

1 How many cameras are available?
The number of available cameras will define how frequently you can cut and how many times you can change shots. The faster the beat the more frequently you may want to cut, but it takes a finite time for a camera to move from one position to another, frame and focus a shot. Pop music cries out for extreme angles, fast camera moves and lens effects. All of them take time as well as skill to achieve.

2 How are the cameras mounted?
One way you certainly cannot shoot music easily is by leaving the cameras in fixed positions as in a current affairs studio, or offering a standard repertoire of shots as in a tennis tournament. In the studio the cameras ought to move. Different camera mountings do different things. The normal studio pedestal is remarkably mobile in expert hands. There are many types of cranes available for high and low shots as well as spectacular tracks. If such mountings are available they need to be used to full effect, otherwise they are just cluttering up precious studio space. They should also be integrated into the rest of the shooting. There is no point in having a crane and then just using it for a single wonderful self-indulgent shot. There is no point in adding a hand-held camera and then leaving it boxed in the second row of the stalls.

3 How mobile can they be?
In the studio the limitations will be imposed by the set, lighting and available floor space. On location the added problem

will be the demands of the event organizers and the players. A paying audience does not want to have cameras chasing around in front of them. Players may object to cameras, even hand-held ones, on the stage. There are a host of fire and safety regulations that may prevent the director putting cameras where he or she might fancy.

4   What are the limitations of set and lighting?

The success of all studio productions depends on the director, designer and lighting supervisor thinking as one. A main problem for a designer is to provide enough backing for the cameras. A string quartet can be shot against simple black drapes; pop groups might actually benefit from shots into the lights.

Strong backlighting and strobe light effects can be spectacular but make it hell for camera operators to keep focus. Designers can help the composition of interesting developing shots by providing foreground interest in the set, but not at the expense of blocking clean shots from other cameras.

> **A word of warning**
> Theatrical stages are not flat. They are raked from front to back, hence the terms upstage and downstage. Cameras need to move fast. Mobile camera mountings are on wheels. There are no safety rails in the front of a proscenium. Work the rest out for yourself.

5   What is the time scale?

Writing the camera script takes time and you will get nowhere without it. Give yourself one hour writing per minute of screen time. In other words you need a clear morning or afternoon for a straightforward number of four minutes or so duration. Studio rehearsal will need time for a minimum of three goes at the music, one to block in the shots and moves with the camera crew, one to try a continuous run according to the camera script to see if it all works (it probably won't) and a third complete rehearsal according to the modified script. This will all take the best part of an hour for our single number.

6   Is there a chance of retakes?

In the case of a studio recording probably yes, in which case build time into the schedule. In the case of a concert almost certainly not. If you are lucky enough to have two bites of the cherry, say a symphony orchestra which does a complete dress rehearsal in the morning and the complete show later, follow the advice for single camera direction and go for the close-ups first. By minimizing the duplication of shots you effectively double the number of cameras. Just be prepared for interminable hours and days of post production.

7 How much post production time is allowed by the budget?

Post production is not an excuse to chuck out camera scripts and planning procedures. All the editing time and cameras in the world will not save an unprepared music recording. If post production is available think of deploying ISO cameras. You still need to plan and rehearse the shots. Just setting ISO cameras loose to see what they can get will be a waste of everybody's time and just multiply the hours in post production.

Once these questions can be answered it is time to start writing camera shots on the script. Keep four principles in mind:

1   Make sure the music is always covered by a basic number of safe shots. Curiously it is much easier during a rehearsal to build in extra shots to the camera script. It is much more difficult to start taking shots out. Last minute removal of shots has a knock-on effect throughout the rest of the camera script. If in doubt remember the maxim KISS (Keep it simple, Stupid).

2   Always keep one camera on any vocalist or soloist when they are performing. This is the real safety shot.

3   Try always to have one wide-angle shot. This need not be a boring wide shot from the back of the hall, though this is not a bad idea with audience shows if a spare camera is available. A wide-angle shot, which need not always be offered by the same camera, is the fail-safe against the moment when the director inadvertently cuts to a non-singing vocalist or non-playing musician.

4   Dedicate one camera to follow the lead vocalist or solo performer. Even if an accompanist or backing

group should be to the fore the lead performer will still be performing or reacting and can legitimately be cut to. Note that to fulfil these minimum conditions properly the director will need four cameras for even a small musical group.

Before putting pencil to paper there is a final creative decision to make. A lot of music will benefit from straight cutting between shots. But music offers all sorts of possibilities for mixes, wipes and digital effects. A staccato rhythm cries out for hard cuts. A slow ballad may demand slow swooping camera moves and mixes between shots. A pacy rock number might be punctuated by digital effects.

Each number should be directed in a consistent style. Lots of cuts but the occasional spectacular couple of tracking shots with a mix or two will look peculiar. Throwing all the video effects on the mixer at one piece of music is just childish, even when the music itself is dismal.

Finally using your imagination to combine the shots which you visualize with the bar breakdown of the script look at a studio floor plan of the set or a sketch plan of the location and start allocating cameras.

1   Show consideration to the camera operators. Ideally the shots would be in sequence, camera one, camera two, camera three, camera four, camera one, camera two and so on. Of course this will not be consistently possible but it is asking for trouble to end a difficult shot on camera two, cut for two bars to camera three and then expect to come back to camera two directly for the start of a quite new shot.

2   Give the fullest description of each shot on the script and, if they are being used, on the camera cards. It will save a lot of rehearsal time.

The final camera script of our ditty will now have become something like this.

1. CAM 1 BCU top hat zoom out to kit	/
2. CAM 3 2S drums and keyboard	2 BARS DRUMS/
3. CAM 4 CU sax bell tilt up	2 BARS DRUMS AND KEYBOARD/
4. CAM 2 WA	2 BARS

5. CAM 3 MS Ld Vocal	SAXOPHONE/ 2 BARS AND TWO BEATS TUTTI/ DAMON
6. Zoom in to MCU	Don't know why
7. CAM 2 MLS profile LV	Don't know where/
8. CAM 1 WA from Cam L TRACK R and Crane up	My baby's gone/
9. CAM 3 BCU Backing V	4 BARS LEAD GUITAR AND DRUMS/ SONIA
10. CAM 4 Low Angle MCU LV	She's away with the fairies/ etc., etc.

Note: cuts best come at the end of something – not at the beginning, except, of course, for the first shot!

Cutting to music is one of the skills in television that comes close to art. A brilliant director and vision mixer do not automatically cut at the end of a line of a lyric or the last beat of a bar. Most cut on the downbeat and some on the upbeat and many will ring the changes in different sections. Some will cut on the last beat of the bar; others half a beat or a beat earlier. A good PA in the gallery will call out the bars for the director and to drive the camera crew.

A fast cutting musical number is in effect driven by the PA and executed by the vision mixer. If the crew is well motivated and properly rehearsed and the camera script works there may be a problem for the actual director to get a word in edgeways.

We have now gone well beyond the beginner stage. Multi camera music recording demands an expert proficiency in the operation of a fully equipped and staffed electronic studio or complex outside broadcast. This is beyond the scope of a simple introductory handbook.

12

Drama notes

Earlier we asserted that all television in essence enacted stories in words and pictures, in other words, drama. Even the hard nosed ex-newspaper men protest in vain when they claim that they seek out and present the unvarnished truth, untainted by the arty-farty conceits of the rest of television. A series of reports from a crisis-torn Balkan republic becomes a narrative, comic or tragic in which the reporters act as a chorus. We listen to politicians on radio and consider the debate. We watch them on television to judge their performances, the squirming evasion, the flush of anger and the dramatic put down of an opponent. Even the nightly weather report is a kind of mini soap opera.

The distinguishing features of television drama pure and simple are that the broadcast is scripted and rehearsed and that it is presented by professional performers. By this definition television drama embraces adaptations of literary works, specially written screenplays, soap opera (called Popular Drama in BBC-speak), most comedy, dramatized documentaries, and a great number of children's programmes. It is not very likely that many readers of this

Figure 12.1

handbook will be looking at the immediate prospect of directing a major costume drama or, for that matter, an episode of a nationally transmitted soap opera. To arrive at this point usually requires an long apprenticeship either on the stage or climbing through the ranks of production management, screenwriting or the cutting rooms. But it is an unusual and unfortunate television director who does not at some point encounter a screenplay to interpret and actors to direct.

There are entire libraries of books on directing drama for the screen and volumes of past screenplays are published. This chapter is addressed not at the film buff who is interested in deconstructing texts or aspires to be the next Peter Greenaway. It simply offers a few basic tips to the sort of beginner coming up against the opportunity to direct some drama or dramatization for the first time.

The screenplay and the writer

If you start with a brilliant script the production will shine despite pedestrian direction and performances. If the script is awful to start with there is very little hope however hard you try to tart up the production values. If you are working with original material you will probably be working with a professional writer. The relationship between the writer and the director is one of what is politely called creative tension. The writer will have strong ideas about the way his or her work should be interpreted, the way lines should be delivered and how scenes should be lit and filmed. The director may have other ideas.

A well-written screenplay should clearly indicate the writer's intentions. Unfortunately there are not too many really good experienced screenwriters around and an awful lot of desperately ambitious inexperienced ones. Even a beginner director should not be shy of asking a writer to change scenes or rewrite lines. Remember the obvious. Television drama is not just a matter of dialogue. The dialogue in a scene may be minimal. A scene of a jail breakout might be full of action and dramatic characterization yet have only monosyllables for words. A dramatized reconstruction of a bank raid for a current affairs documentary may have no real dialogue at all. Inexperienced writers tend to overwrite.

The director's job is to interpret the screenplay on the page and bring it to life. Some writers will insist on being present throughout the rehearsal period and even turning up at the filming days. This can be a great advantage when last minute rewrites are called for either because the actors feel a need to alter lines or there are practical difficulties like a need to shorten a piece or change the action on account of the location. It can also be a pain if the director has to keep referring to the writer about interpretation. If both are inexperienced, keep to two simple ground rules:

1   The director and actors have no right to alter the writer's screenplay without consultation.
2   The director is totally in charge of the cameras and the crew. The writer may not go behind the director's back to talk directly to actors or the cameraman.

There are times when there is no professional writer. Occasions arise when the budget and time do not a allow for one. The director may have to write everything from scratch, perhaps a documentary reconstruction, perhaps a comic sketch. A truly nightmare scenario arises in corporate videos where business clients not only decide that they want dramatization but want to write the lines as well. The director then has to take personal responsibility for a complete rewrite.

Casting

Get the casting right and half your remaining problems are over. Corporate clients in particular often propose that to cut costs non-professionals should be employed. Do not be tempted. There are few more depressing experiences than trying to get a real fireman to act being shocked by a car crash or a real manager to perform in a scripted mock interview. The local amateur dramatic society will be no better. An acclaimed performance as Widow Twankey is no recommendation for a tense scene shot in close-up. There are agreements, very restricting ones, about the use of drama students and children from stage schools. With even a very modest budget though these expedients should not be necessary.

Britain is uniquely blessed by the numbers and quality of its actors. All of them are represented by British Actors' Equity which negotiates minimum fees and conditions of employment. Assuming that the director is fresh to drama and has not the support of an experienced production manager or first assistant director he or she will have to do the casting unaided. There are two main approaches.

1   Trawl through one or two of the leading theatrical agents, state what you need and what you can afford and ask if they can assist from the actors on their books. If the production is a dramatic reconstruction and looks are as important as delivery this can be a quick and easy solution, but you will be buying a bit of a pig in a poke; on the other hand agents may welcome a chance to try out excellent performers who are newly on the books, or have not worked in a while. Try to audition them before agreeing to anything.

2   Look through the pages of *Spotlight*, the directory of almost all British actors and actresses. *Spotlight* has photographs, professional CVs, and details of agents. Even if the resources are very limited the director ought not to be shy about approaching well-known performers. Acting is the most insecure of professions. An actor whose face may seem to be on every TV channel may have been classified as 'overexposed' by casting directors and not have worked at all for the previous 12 months!

Some actors, and their agents, get very concerned about their image in the profession and will only deign to take plum roles for high fees. But many others would rather work at anything rather than sit at home waiting for the telephone to ring. A lot will depend on your product. Working on an interesting project for a film school or for an up and coming director on an obscure series might be a good investment for the future. It might get more work, it might make an interesting addition to a CV or show reel. A really dull training video for a factory will probably command a high fee.

Auditions

If it is possible audition your artists. Let them have copies of the screenplay or a scene of the script well in advance. Discuss the production with them in detail and ask their opinions about the role being offered. An enthusiastic performer will have worked out a tentative interpretation. An uninterested one will just wait for the director to tell him or her precisely what to do. Do not assume that the agent has given the performer much of a briefing. Get the actor to read through a few pages of script, with yourself reading the other parts. You will soon know if you have the right person. If you are lucky this will be the first time that the words will leap from the page and be present there in flesh and blood. If the performance is just not right, even though the actor is well established, do not hesitate to look elsewhere. Actors are all used to auditioning, and to the disappointment of not getting a part. A problem may arise from geography. London is awash with available actors and actresses. If the production is based in the distant provinces the production may have to make do with a very limited selection of artistes. A well-heeled casting director will hire London premises and conduct auditions there. London-based performers though will naturally expect considerable travelling and location expenses in addition to the fee. It might be an advantage to investigate which performers are resident or available in the region in question.

A word of warning

The director should normally make all approaches through an agent. Not all actors are represented by agents, however. Agents are also in the business of keeping up the fees of their clients. If you have personal contacts, or are completely set upon a particular performer, it can be worthwhile making a direct personal approach, outlining the project and if possible sending a script. But be careful not to make any offer until you are certain about your choice. The first approach always should be an availability check only. If you ask if Dame Peggy would be available between certain dates well and good. If you start by asking Dame Peggy if she would play Lady Macbeth on such and such days you will have offered a verbal contract. If subsequently you decide that you cannot afford the Dame, or postpone the production and Dame Peggy has subsequently turned down other work, you will be liable to pay cancellation fees.

> **Word of warning**
> Outside the London region there are numbers of available extras (supporting artistes or walk-ons as they are variously known). Most are represented by Equity although there are agreements that where Equity members are not available members of the general public may be contracted for the same fees. Extras come cheaper than featured actors, but not a great deal so. There are strictly defined limits to what an extra may be directed to do. What they may definitely not do is deliver any lines of directed dialogue. The director may ask a crowd to shout and cheer or make improvised mutterings at a bus stop but not be asked to say 'This is a hold up!' in a bank raid scene. On balance it is better and safer to employ proper actors and actresses. You may not employ an actor as an extra or vice versa.

Rehearsals

No two directors work in the same way. The British director Mike Leigh begins with the merest outline of a screenplay and allows the characterization and plot to develop over many months of rehearsal and improvisation. The Italian director Antonioni was notorious for not telling his artists anything about the motivation for their characters' actions. Reputedly the stars only discovered what their films were all about when they went to the cinema. For most television directors the opportunities for rehearsal are limited. Pressure of deadlines, availability of actors and access to locations as well as financial constraints make this inevitable.

Multi camera studio drama has to be rehearsed and plotted meticulously like any other kind of production. But little drama today is shot properly as multicamera. Even in fast turnaround soaps where two or three cameras are used the shooting tends to be broken down scene by scene or sequence by sequence and then edited. Most directors with a theatrical background prefer to work on the studio floor with their performers and effectively work a shot at a time as though they were directing a single film camera. The days of live studio drama are gone. So whether the shoot involves a studio set or an outside location it is unlikely that there will be time for much rehearsal on site. Ideally the director should go through a minimum number of steps.

The read-through

The only way actors can get a feel of the way their performances interrelate will be by reading through the script with the director and writer. It would help if one of these has provided biographical details for the characters along with the script. If the writer has envisaged a gardener as being an illiterate rustic simpleton and this is not self-evident from the dialogue, a biographical sketch is needed. It will be frustrating for all if an actor turns up prepared to play Mellors from *Lady Chatterley's Lover*. The director needs to let the actors interact, make suggestions and offer bits of 'business' to strengthen their performances. It will not be helpful to start laying down the law about every detail from the start. The writer should also stand back and only contribute when there are obvious difficulties with lines or situations. As performances gel the writer will probably spot emerging subtexts which were never imagined before. Some actors will give fulsome performances at the read-through but most will keep things very low key. Do not worry. Performers will often not give their all until in front of the camera.

Blocking the shots

The read-through should develop into the performance of entire scenes complete with moves. It is important that there is an indication of the set or location from the director. Improvisation is the name of the game. Any old chairs and tables or packing cases can stand in for furniture. What the cast needs to know is the dimensions and position of important objects. It has to be clear where doors and windows are situated. If the designer can provide a floor plan the rehearsal area can be marked with coloured tape to designate the area and layout of the set. From this point the director must think in terms of cameras. Theatrical directors who come fresh to television sometimes have a mental block. They are used to directing performances from a favoured position, often the second row of the stalls, but the television director's place is where an imaginary camera is looking at the action from the various possible angles. Experienced actors will also appreciate knowing which camera position the director intends to use so that moves can be modified.

It is now the time to see whether both performance and shots can be improved by moving furniture and properties. The more time spent blocking and rehearsing the better will be the dramatic timing of the performers and the fewer will be the problems of continuity on the shooting day. There are a dozen ways in which an actor can walk to a table and pick up a telephone. A couple of walk-throughs will discover the appropriate action and timing. The actor will get this right time and again. If this is left to last minute improvisation the chances are that the number of steps, the facial expression and the position of the hands will change between a wide-angle shot and any subsequent close-ups.

The location recce

Everything written earlier about the importance of the recce applies to drama with the need for even greater attention to detail. An expensive production will have its own location manager and there may be several recces involving the designer and special effects organizer, the lighting cameraman, the production manager and maybe a safety officer. A modest production may limit the recce to the director and perhaps one assistant. The director should try always to make two recces, the first to solve all the usual practical problems and make initial decisions about where and how to shoot, the second in the company of the cameraman/woman. The quality of a production can be made or broken by the quality of the lighting. The lighting cameraman needs to know the potential of the location, the mood of a scene and the director's shooting plans, only then can the appropriate number and types of lamps be ordered for the shoot. Letting the location be a surprise for the camera crew may save one day's cameraman's wages. There then will have to be even more expensive shooting time wasted with discussing lighting and setting up the shots. The more precise the information about the location the more accurate can be the blocking of shots in the rehearsals.

Shooting

The complex subject of the relationship between the director and the cast is not one for this simple handbook, nor are the technical matters of lighting and camerawork. The thing about television drama is that it is the most difficult and the most rewarding television genre. Because of this everyone, actors and crew, tend to give of their very professional best. Drama is exciting and it is fun. If the atmosphere on set is unhappy and the production a mess this will be almost always due to the incompetence or arrogance of the director. Even if your previous dramatic experience has been the School Play you can still succeed on television by following some simple tips.

Ten helpful hints

1   Draw up a schedule for every shooting day. Never try to achieve more than the time allows. Individual shots take time to set up and light. Performers need time to get into their roles. They also need time for rest as well as time with costume and make-up. If shooting over several days try to make the first day as simple as possible. Remember most of the people involved will have met for the first time. A certain formula for creating a poisonous atmosphere is for the director to start out shooting at a gallop on day one so that professional standards are compromised, and then to hand out blame for any over-runs or flaws in performance.

2   Work as closely as possible with the lighting cameraman or woman. The director should discuss the daily schedule and take technical advice about what can be achieved. A decent cameraman will often be able to advise on how to cut down on the number of set-ups, or substitute simple for complex shots. But employ a real lighting cameraman, not a current affairs style camera operator. Drama demands creative and sensitive photography.

3   Let the actors perform the complete scene. This is both to familiarize themselves with their moves and dramatic timing, and for the technical crew to watch. Last minute changes to props, lights and camera angles can then be carried out quickly before a take. There is a risk that the director gets so carried away with the technical detail of shots and cameras that the actors are treated like mere puppets.

4   Always overlap dialogue and action. If a performer is to deliver a single line in close-up ask the performers out of vision to deliver the previous lines of dialogue and, if there is to be a reaction, the subsequent line. But never forget editing problems. Actors on a single camera shoot must never talk over each other's lines. Overlap action at all times. If the performer is to sit down and light a pipe in both long shot and close-up make sure the complete action is repeated both times, even if the original intention is to cut on the lighting of the match rather than the sitting movement. Things may change in the cutting room.

5   Beware of cutting from two-shot to two-shot. In a multi camera studio you can get away with this because you are shooting in real time and there can be no continuity errors (the shots may be ugly nonetheless). The wider the two-shots on single camera the greater the risk of one of the performers making a continuity mistake and the more likely the appearance of a jump cut. Remember the rules which apply when selecting shots for interviews and discussions. The only difference is that with drama you have rehearsed the lines in advance and can plan accordingly.

6   Plan the shots, do not shoot unnecessarily. The trap for the insecure director is to go for a 'safety' shot by shooting an entire scene in a fixed wide-angle framing first. This is the equivalent of the studio interview director who ties up a camera throughout on a studio wide shot which only has any use at the very beginning and end of the item. Subsequent shots of the action recorded as developing shots, two-shots and close-ups will make the original wide angle redundant. Sod's Law will dictate that the continuity differences between the wide angle and the close-ups will be horrendous. If the shoot is badly planned or so pushed for time that the editor is obliged to keep cutting back to the wide angle in mid-scene the shot will appear as obvious a cutaway as a noddy or audience shot in a current affairs show. The static wide safety shot is not to be confused with a scene shot on a single camera as one continuous developing shot. The latter needs a lot

of skill and rehearsal and the camera will need a suitable mounting whether a dolly and jib arm or a trained steadicam operator.

7   Think parallel actions. Dramatic tension is built by the ability of the film director to compress or stretch time and the surest way to achieve this is to intercut between two parallel scenes. Tension is created for instance, by intercutting the shots of an actress bathing and getting ready to go out and a hand opening a drawer to take out a razor and feet slowly climbing the stairs. The oldest film gag intercuts between the fat man walking down the street and the comic peeling a banana and throwing away the skin. A dialogue scene in the back of a taxi might be intercut with a shot of the preparations for the reception (or the planting of a bomb) at the destination.

Even where there is no obvious simultaneous action the director can create similar dramatic pacing by cutting within a scene. For example, a scene in a railway carriage can be intercut with a wide angle of the train steaming through the countryside, or wheels passing by or over the camera, or even a shot of the station clock at the terminus.

These are all planned shots to enable the proper pacing of the drama, they are *not* cutaways to dig the director out of trouble. Any good writer will indicate parallel action and intercut scenes in the screenplay. If these are not sufficiently indicated it is up to the director to create them.

8   Keep sets and shooting simple. The viewer only sees what the director wants the viewer to see. There is no virtue in creating a reality which is not shown or is irrelevant particularly if time and cash are at a premium. If there is a brief scene in a hotel bedroom there is absolutely no reason to hire a room in a real hotel when the scene only involves a man sitting on a bed to unpack a case or make a phone call. A bedside lamp, a prop telephone and maybe a standard hotel coffee making kit on a bedside table is all that is needed to convey the message 'hotel room'. This can be mocked up almost anywhere.

A brilliant evocation of New York in the 1940s can be achieved in Birmingham by shooting at night with a couple of period cars, feet wearing spats passing through puddles, a few fedora hats and a lot of steam coming up gratings. Los Angeles circa 1935 is easily evoked by flashing a red light through a venetian blind, showing a period stick telephone and lettering on a glass door against the sound of police sirens. A lot of nonsense has been talked lately by programme executives about 'production values'. This involves blowing the budget on sumptuous frocks, packing unnecessary street exteriors with vintage cars, or hiring a harbour with boats, rain and smoke effects for a two-shot against a quayside wall which could as well be shot at the nearest canal lock.

9   Motivate the cuts by movement. Use actions to reinforce dialogue. Most dialogue sequences could be shot entirely in close-ups. In reality people often do not move much when engaged in conversation or argument. On the small screen constant close-ups rapidly pall. The viewer has no visual clue to the physical relationship of the actors to each other. The skilled director builds in physical movements to give a meaningful motivation for camera moves and cutting points.

Movements may be as large as one character crossing behind another or one rising as another sits or as small as raising a glass to the lips or lighting a cigarette. This need not entail the performers pacing about like caged lions. Unlike stage performances motivation on television can be provided in close-up by as little as a raised eyebrow or a slight head turn. But the cues have to be planned and directed. Changes of eyelines, camera heights and lens angles all contribute to the dramatic effect.

10   Remember sound. Our evocation of Los Angeles was completed by a distant police siren, the tension of our railway carriage scene could be emphasized by a shock cut to the train roaring out of a tunnel to the scream of a steam whistle. The tension or eroticism of our scene with the actress getting dressed would be strengthened by the sounds of the shower and close-

ups with exaggerated sound of zips being undone and the rustle of silk contrasting with the creak of the footsteps on the stairs.

Wonders can be performed with sound in post production. In feature films the whole sound track, including the dialogue, may be a creation of sound dubbing. In low budget television it pays to record as much and as good quality sound as possible on location. Sound as well as movement can motivate cuts. The ring of the telephone and the knock on the door may be clichés but they are ever useful for a change of scene or alteration of mood.

To conclude and bring us back to the very beginning, remember that the skills needed to make a lively four-minute magazine story are the same as those demanded by a lavish costume drama. The scale may be different but there is no fundamental difference between the one type of direction and the other. It all depends on the wits and knowledge of the director.

The crucial moment in *Othello* is the scene where Iago winds up the jealousy of the Moor by hinting at the infidelity of Desdemona. Orson Welles shot it in a Turkish bath. This author has listened to a lot of film studies blather about the symbolism and semiotics of the scene, the oriental exoticism of the location, the racial implications, the use of steam to convey murky treachery or even suggest a homosexual sub-text. Actually the costumes had been impounded by the Italian customs. Welles only had the actors contracted for a few days and, like almost every director in television today, had almost no cash. The actors wore only towels because towels were all there were to wear. And a Turkish bath opened up all sorts of possibilities for interesting camera angles and dramatic lighting. Sod's Law was turned to spectacular advantage. That's real directing.

Appendix

Shooting interviews and discussions

A rough distinction between a studio interview and a discussion is that an interview is shot with as many cameras as there are guests; a discussion implies more guests, often many more, than there are cameras. Discussions are therefore the more complex to direct. This does not mean that an interview director ought to lock off the cameras one to a performer. As the previous chapters should have made clear there is an art to directing even the simplest of formats.

No two interviews or discussions are identical and no two skilled directors would shoot in exactly the same way. The following seating arrangements and possible camera shots are well-tested formulae for the most commonly met studio situations. It is not suggested that the director try to incorporate each of these shots or camera positions in a single production but to propose workable possibilities.

When the diagrams concern discussions the initial camera positions are marked; the inventive director may discover others. A lot depends on the set design and the way a discussion is structured as well as the flexibility of the camera mountings. Never forget that in a professional studio the cameras can move. When planning an interview or discussion remember the cardinal rules:

1   Cross shoot to get the best possible eyelines but be careful not to cross the line in discussions.

2   Position the cameras so that composition and lens angles will match.

3   Choose a seating plan appropriate to the subject matter and role of the participants.

4   Use two-shots and wide shots to establish the geography of the set. Do not leave the viewers confused about who is talking to whom.

5   Always have a safety shot available and think two shots ahead.

6   Watch all the camera monitors. The commonest disasters arise when a director fails to notice that all the cameras offer almost identical shots leaving nowhere to cut when a surprise interjection happens.

Interviews – suggested seating plans

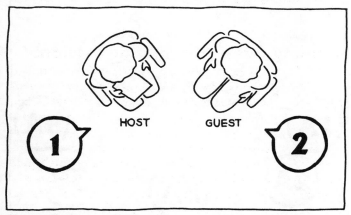

Two cameras on a 1+1

Camera 1 shots	Camera 2 shots
• 2s favouring guest	• 2s favouring host
• MS guest	• MS host
• MCU guest	• MCU host
• CU guest	• CU host

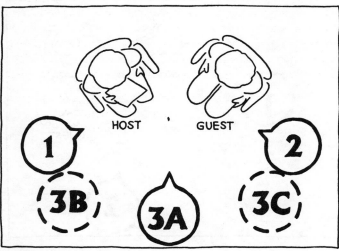

Three cameras on a 1+1
Camera 3 shots
- Any 2s
- Profiles of guest
- Profiles of host

Four cameras on a 1+1
Camera 3 shots
- NB Camera 3 has been given 2 positions and not Camera 2
- This is because it is always more important to favour the guest

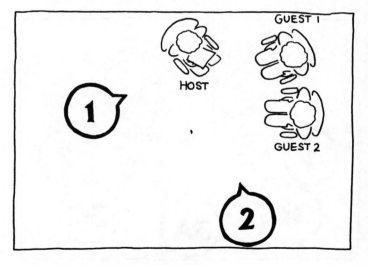

Two cameras on a 1+2, host on side

Camera 1 shots
- 2s guests 1 and 2
- MS, MCU, CU guest 1
- MS, MCU, CU guest 2

Camera 2 shots
- 3s host, guests 1 and 2
- 2s guests 1 and 2
- MS, MCU, CU host

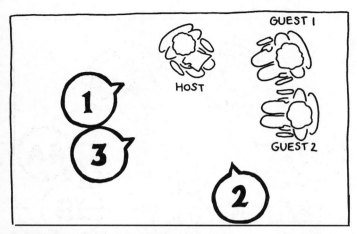

Three cameras on a 1+2, host on side

Camera 1 shots
- 3s group
- MS, MCU, CU guest 1
- MS, MCU, CU guest 2
- 2s guests 1 and 2

Camera 2 shots
- 3s group
- MS, MCU, CU host
- 2s guests 1 and 2
- MS, MCU, CU guest 1

Camera 3 shots
- 2s guests 1 and 2
- MS, MCU, CU guest 1
- MS, MCU, CU guest 2
- 3s group

Two cameras on a 1+2, host in centre

Camera 1A shots
- 3s group
- 2s left host and guest 1
- MS, MCU, CU guest 2
- MS, MCU, CU host

Camera 2 shots
- 3s group
- 2s right host and guest 2
- MS, MCU, CU guest 1
- MS, MCU, CU host

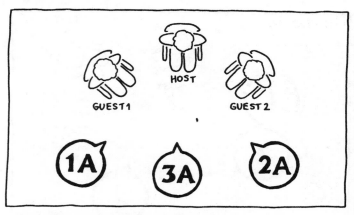

Three cameras on a 1+2, host in centre

Camera 1 shots
- MS, MCU, CU guest 2

Camera 2 shots
- MS, MCU, CU guest 1

Camera 3 shots
- 3s group
- MS, MCU, CU host
- 2s right, guest 2 and host
- 2s leftt, guest 1 and host

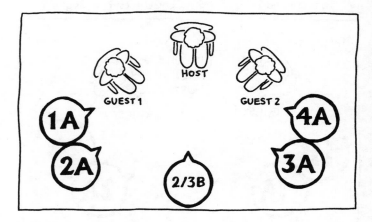

Four cameras on a 1+2, host in centre

Camera 1 shots
- MS, MCU, CU guest 2

Camera 3 shots
- 3s group
- MS, MCU, CU host
- 2s right, guest 2 and host
- Possibly MCU guest 1

Camera 2 shots
- 3s group
- 2s left, guest 1 and host
- MS, MCU, CU host
- Possibly MCU guest 2

Camera 4 shots
- MS, MCU, CU guest 1

Discussions

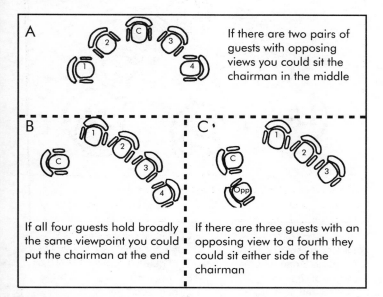

A — If there are two pairs of guests with opposing views you could sit the chairman in the middle

B — If all four guests hold broadly the same viewpoint you could put the chairman at the end

C — If there are three guests with an opposing view to a fourth they could sit either side of the chairman

Discussion with four guests

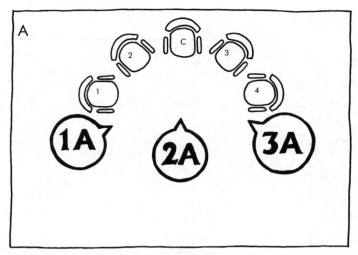

Camera 1 can get
Singles of guests 3 and 4
2s of guests 3 and 4
* Singles of chair to
   guest 3 and guest 4
* 5s and 3s left
* 2s left guest 2 to guest 1

Camera 2 can get
Singles of chairman
2s of guests 1 and 2,
chairman and guest 2
2s of guests 3 and 4,
chairman and guest 3
3s left
3s right

Camera 3 can get
Singles of guests 1 and 2
2s of guests 1 and 2
* Singles of chair to guest 3 and guest 4
* 5s and 3s right
* 2s guest 3 to guest 4

* These shots will mean moving off the eyeline

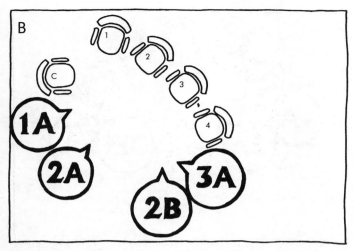

Camera 1 can get
Singles of all guests
Any 2s of guests (L, R, or C)
Any 3s of guests (L or R)
4s of guests

Camera 3 can get
Singles of chairman
5s (by crabbing L a little)

Camera 2 can get
(By crabbing L or R)
All of camera 1's shots
(Eyelines will not be as good so use
2 wide and 1 close as a rule)
5S

Camera 1 can get
Singles of all guests
2s of guests (L & R)
3s of guests
5s (possible by moving
slightly right)

Camera 2 can get
(By crabbing L or R to
improve eyelines)
WA/5s
Singles of chairman
4sR
2sL

Camera 3 can get
Singles of oppo
Singles of chairman
2s L
4s R

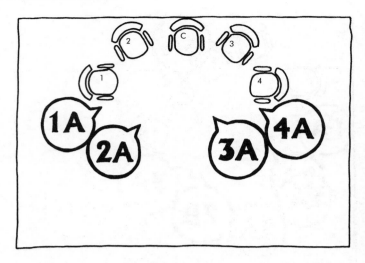

Discussion with four cameras

Camera 1 can get
Singles of guest 3 and guest 4
2s of guest 3 and guest 4
Possible tight 5s

Camera 2 can get
WA/5s
Singles of chair looking L
3sL
2s of guest 1 and guest 2
2s of guest 3 and guest 4
Singles of guest 3 and guest 4

Camera 3 can get
WA/5s
Singles of chair looking R
2s of guest 3 and guest 4
2s of guest 1 and guest 2
Singles of guest 1 and guest 2

Camera 4 can get
Singles of guest 1 and guest 2
2s of guest 1 and guest 2
Possible tight 5s

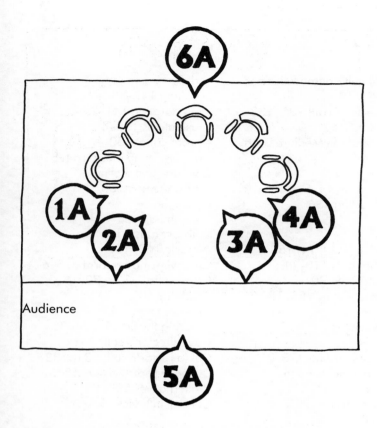

Audience

Discussion with audience participation and six cameras

INDEX

LIBRARY
ST. LOUIS COMMUNITY COLLEGE
AT FLORISSANT VALLEY.